SO, YOU WANT TO BE A WRITER?

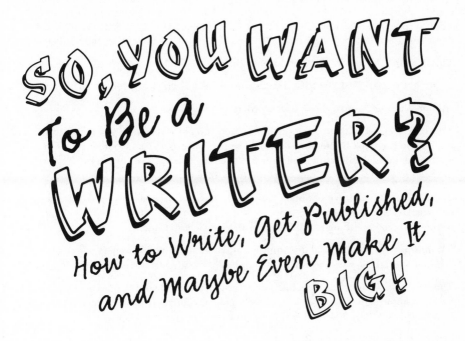

SO, YOU WANT TO BE A WRITER?

How to Write, Get Published, and Maybe Even Make It BIG!

by Vicki Hambleton &
Cathleen Greenwood

ALADDIN
New York London Toronto Sydney New Delhi

BEYOND WORDS
Hillsboro, Oregon

ALADDIN
An imprint of Simon & Schuster
Children's Publishing Division
1230 Avenue of the Americas
New York, NY 10020

BEYOND WORDS
20827 N.W. Cornell Road, Suite 500
Hillsboro, Oregon 97124-9808
503-531-8700 / 503-531-8773 fax
www.beyondword.com

This Aladdin/Beyond Words edition May 2012

For information about special discounts for bulk purchases, please contact Simon & Schuster Special Sales at 1-866-506-1949 or business@simonandschuster.com.

The Simon & Schuster Speakers Bureau can bring authors to your live event. For more information or to book an event contact the Simon & Schuster Speakers Bureau at 1-866-248-3049 or visit our website at www.simonspeakers.com.

Managing Editor: Lindsay S. Brown
Copyeditor: Sheila Ashdown
Proofreader: Gretchen Stelter
Design: Sara E. Blum
The text of this book was set in Bembo.

Manufactured in the United States of America 1015 FFG

10 9 8 7 6 5 4 3 2

Library of Congress Cataloging-in-Publication Data

Hambleton, Vicki.
    So, you want to be a writer? : how to write, get published, and maybe even make
    it big! / Vicki Hambleton, Cathleen Greenwood.
        p   cm.
    Rev. ed. of: So, you wanna be a writer?
    1. Authorship—Juvenile literature. 2. Authorship—Marketing—Juvenile literature.
    3. Authorship—Vocational guidance—Juvenile literature. I. Greenwood,
    Cathleen. II. Hambleton, Vicki. III. Title. So, you wanna be a writer?
    PN159.H28 2012
    808.02—dc23
                                                                            2011046252

ISBN 978-1-58270-353-4 (pbk)
ISBN 978-1-58270-359-6 (hc)
ISBN 978-1-4424-5291-6 (eBook)

CONTENTS

Chapter 1
What's It Like to Be a Writer? 1

Chapter 2
Getting Started with the "Write" Stuff:
Time, Tools, and Turf 11

Chapter 3
Poetry, Fiction, Sci-Fi, and More:
Exploring the Different Genres 29

Chapter 4
Choosing Your Topic: What Will You Write About? 49

Chapter 5
Writing Exercises: How to Get Unstuck Fast 57

Chapter 6
The Process: Writing and Rewriting 79

Chapter 7
You've Written Your Masterpiece: Now What?
Let Them Read It! 97

Chapter 8
How to Get Published: Creating a Proposal 125

Chapter 9
Getting Published: *What to Do If They Say No—*
What to Do If They Say Yes! 139

Chapter 10
Writing as a Career: *You Mean I Can Get Paid for That?* 151

Chapter 11
Resources for Writers 163

Chapter 12
Glossary: *Words That Writers, Publishers, and Teachers*
Use a Lot—And What They Mean! 179

About the Authors 186

1

What's It Like to Be a Writer?

You pull into the parking lot of your favorite bookstore, knowing that this time it's not going to be just to meet your buddies. Someone else is expecting you—YOUR FANS! You keep your sunglasses on as you walk in the front door, head down, but the manager recognizes you anyway. You try to finish your last call as you are whisked away to the greenroom, offered your favorite drink, and escorted to the book signing table. It's covered with a red velvet cloth, piled high with copies of YOUR book, and there are scores of fans jostling for position behind the velvet ropes to make sure they get their books signed by the author—YOU!

Cameras flash, your smile dazzles. You whip out your favorite pen and start signing as fast as you can, murmuring words of gratitude in response to the exclamations of love and adulation from each reader.

Is this what it's like to be a writer? You bet! Okay, maybe it's not *always* like this—but it does happen. And, believe it or not, it can happen to you, especially if you start thinking of yourself as a writer now and doing the things real writers do. This book will help you—we promise.

Keep that thrilling, ultimate scenario in mind, but let's get a bit more realistic for a few minutes. Look over the list below and circle what you really think it's like to be a writer.

1. lonely
2. cool
3. strange
4. incredibly exciting
5. hard work
6. not like real work at all
7. boring
8. a life of riches
9. a life of poverty
10. people love you
11. people think you're a geek
12. fun
13. frustrating
14. fantastic
15. scary
16. hilarious
17. eeeyew!

Let's see what you think about writing:

- If you circled just even numbers (2, 4, 6, 8, etc.), we love you! You have a positive attitude about writing. And you're right…being a writer *can* be all of those things! (Although, to be honest, not *all* the time.)

- If you circled just odd numbers (1, 3, 5, 7, etc.), you're right too. Being a writer can be tough, but it's *never* as bad as that whole list. At least, not if you read this book first!

- If you circled all the items on the list, you are right on target—being a writer is often like *all* of these things at one point or another.

How One Author Got His Start

Michael Crichton's books have sold over 150 million copies. In 1994, Crichton became the only creative artist ever to have works on the bestseller lists in television, movies, and books (with *ER*, *Jurassic Park*, and *Disclosure*, respectively). Believe it or not, the creator of *Jurassic Park* and *ER* first got published when he was a kid. We conducted the interview below in 2001. He passed away in 2008.

When did you know you wanted to be a writer?

My father was a journalist, so I grew up seeing him type to earn a living. His example made writing seem like a normal thing to do. I was attracted to writing from an early age and did a lot of it. I wrote for my high school and town newspapers, and for the college newspaper. Later on, in medical school, I started writing novels to pay my way through school.

I was fourteen years old when I published my first piece. On a family vacation I visited Sunset Crater Volcano National Monument in Arizona, and I thought it was pretty interesting and that more people should know about it. My parents said that the Sunday *New York Times* travel section published articles by readers and suggested I write an article for the paper. So I sent in an essay—and they published it. I was very excited.

What advice would you give a young writer?

I always tell writers to write. If you think you're interested in writing, just start writing. Write extra compositions for school assignments. Write for the school paper, the yearbook, or the town newspaper. Write articles. Write poetry. Write plays. Write anything you have a mind to, but write a lot.

This will help you learn how to do it—I believe writers are invariably self-taught. But equally important, you'll also find out if you really like writing as much as you think you do. Although writing can be very satisfying, it's a hard job, and a peculiar one. You've got to be self-disciplined, and you've got to tolerate being alone a lot. It's a great life, but it's not for everyone.

If you like to write, you are one of the luckiest people in the world. Writers shape thoughts into words, and those words can inspire, motivate, teach, and entertain those who read them. Have you ever read something that made you cry? *If I Stay, Walk Two Moons,* or *Charlotte's Web*? Or maybe a story in a magazine about a terrible famine? How about something that made you angry? Scared? Happy? How about a book that you just couldn't put down and had to finish under the covers long after midnight ... perhaps a Harry Potter tale?

All of these stories started with writers. There are as many different kinds of writers as there are stories to tell. Writers don't just write books either. When you watch ESPN to catch the sports scores, the reporters on those shows read scripts written by writers. Or when you watch your favorite sitcom, a writer did that as well. The words you read in advertisements and hear in the audio for video games were all carefully chosen by writers. There are novelists, bloggers, poets, playwrights, screenwriters, reporters, medical writers, copywriters, and technical writers, just to name a few. And the good news is that you can make a living as a writer. Your writing can take you all over the world if you choose, or you can create books in the comfort of your own home—even in your pj's if you want!

Young Author Profile:
Juli Weiner

Twenty-three-year-old **Juli Weiner** graduated from Barnard, a liberal arts college affiliated with Columbia University, and works as a blogger for the magazine *Vanity Fair*.

When did you know you wanted to be a writer?
I've wanted to write professionally since middle school. I had

become obsessed with early episodes of *Saturday Night Live* (1975–1980), and used to write comedy sketches in journals and take down notes while watching reruns on TV. Initially I was much more interested in screenwriting than journalism. After writing a satirical column for my high school paper, though, I came around to the idea that journalism and nonfiction writing could be just as colorful, voicey, and fun as creating characters.

What do you like to write the most and why?
My favorite type of writing to do—and, luckily, the type of writing I do most frequently—is political satire. I love following the news, sifting through sound bites to pinpoint something particularly absurd, and taking a faulty line of reasoning to its logical conclusion.

What are your goals for your writing future?
I'd love to challenge myself by doing longer pieces that involve more investigative reporting. As a blogger, I'm often strapped for time and don't get to include as many details in my pieces, interviews, and research as I would be able to if I wrote for a weekly or monthly magazine. I also would love to do a story that involves sneaking around, using a flashlight, or wearing a disguise.

What was your first published piece (and format) and how did you feel?
My first professional published piece was a chart comparing the Palin and Kardashian families that appeared in the February 2011 issue of *Vanity Fair*. I was elated to see my name—and picture and biography, in the contributors section!—in print. *Vanity Fair* is a magazine I've admired since I was old enough to read, and it was beyond incredible to be included alongside the best living journalists and photographers. I felt a huge sense of accomplishment, pride, and relief—similar to what I imagine a physically painless version of childbirth might feel like.

Where else have you been published?
I've written a few pieces for *Vanity Fair* and write several smaller

pieces a day for their website. I've also written for *Wonkette*, *The Huffington Post*, Vice.com, Radar.com, and *The Awl*.

Do you write full-time, and, if not, would you like to? What would be your dream job?

I am lucky enough to write full-time. Barring the possibility of taking a time machine to the late '80s to write for *Spy* magazine, cofounded by *Vanity Fair* editor Graydon Carter, I can't imagine a job better suited to my interests, strengths, and goals than my current one.

What advice would you give to a young writer?

Don't worry about trying to write in the style of someone who's already published or successful—that niche is already occupied! Just write however *you* write best. In terms of landing a job: keep in touch with everyone and be kind to everyone. Don't get nervous when people your age get an earlier career bump than you; if you're good, it won't be long until someone takes notice.

And one bit of practical advice: back up *everything*. It's a law of physics that computers break at precisely the most inopportune time.

Do you think reading helps your writing?

Absolutely. I'm a voracious reader of novels. The best journalism is as compelling and fluid as fiction, so just having an understanding of the way people tell stories and introduce characters (even if they're not real people) is essential. I tend to be a completist: I try to read *everything* by Philip Roth, then everything by Martin Amis, and so on.

What are your favorite reads?

I read *The New Yorker* and *New York* every week, and *Vanity Fair* and *GQ* every month.

Name some of the authors who have inspired you and why.

I read a ton of political blogs and have really taken so many cues from the deadpan incredulity of Alex Pareene at Salon.com, the unbelievably hilarious Jim Newell at Gawker.com, and *Wonkette* owner Ken Layne's moral barometer.

If you like to write, you can use your talent to try lots of different things. All it takes is a desire to write and pen and paper—or a laptop. Throughout the book, you'll hear from lots of different kinds of writers, including writers your age, about what they do, how they got there, and why they love writing.

What's Next for You?

What do the following writers have in common?

Sylvia Plath
James Joyce
Edgar Allan Poe
Langston Hughes
F. Scott Fitzgerald
Louisa May Alcott
Ernest Hemingway
Walt Whitman
Stephen King
Cameron Crowe
S. E. Hinton
Christopher Paolini
Kate Griffin
Amanda Hocking

If you guessed that they were all published writers while they were teenagers, you're right! They didn't wait until they were adults to go for their dreams, and you don't need to either. Add your name to this list! There are so many kinds of writing to try and so many ways to get published as a kid, why wait?

Inspired yet? Read on and find out how you can get started right now!

Young Author Profile:
Victoria Ford

As a high school senior **Victoria Ford** was presented with a scholarship and a Scholastic Art and Writing Award, an honor previously won by Truman Capote, Joyce Carol Oates, and Sylvia Plath.

Seventeen-year-old Victoria Ford feels that writing is a healing process and credits her family as the inspiration for much of her work. An admirer of poet Larry Levis and memoirist Abigail Thomahe, Victoria plans to leave her hometown, Greenville, South Carolina, to attend the University of Pennsylvania.

Like an Event Horizon
Personal Essay/Memoir

Except I wouldn't have quite used those words the summer my older brother Theo left Hickory Ridge. Maybe because I didn't know enough about science or the sky to mark that night as something close to a phenomenon, some boundary in space time. But a summer like that: after a windstorm in June uprooted a magnolia tree and it soaked in the neighborhood pool for over a month, hurting the feelings of a few chubby Hispanic children who lived in my building, so much so that they would experience small bouts of rage, tossing fallen walnuts, balls of laundry lint, broken toys, and their own tennis shoes across the pool's fence, screaming sheepishly to their mothers "Fix it, Fix it. Mama, we're hot and sticky and the bathtub at home is no more fun."

And there was Midnight, my neighbor's black German shepherd, howling until sunrise on some mornings. Maybe he was starving. Maybe he was hurting from the chain that kept him incarcerated in the supply closet. And there was the yellow caution tape wrapped around our stairwell after the middle-aged couple in the flat upstairs ended the week with another fistfight— over a lost key or a missed call or whatever it took to turn people against the ones they loved. There was all of that, everything that made each of us in Apartment 75 a little more lonesome in the Carolina heat, a little more miserable.

It's been a year since Theo left and the air conditioner in almost every apartment this week is broken. It's hot. Actually, it's more than one hundred degrees outside, but if you're in here with me, watching my younger brother, Johnjohn, water a pile of leaves in the living room, you're wishing you were in his hands, because the beads of sweat forming above your lip make your body thirst more than anything has before. I feel as though everything is beginning to take on more weight. The kitchen wallpaper unbuttons itself from the corners, rolling slowly toward the center, and the leaves on my mother's banana plant on the windowsill sag to the floor like the neck of a swan.

My mother woke early this morning, tearing through the house and knocking over picture frames in the narrow spine of our hallway. She remembers—of course she remembers. Just last year on this day, she claimed Theo "divorced from the family forever." I figured she felt the same angst, maybe even heartache, I had when he told me his secret: how he planned to hitch a ride back to Memphis because he couldn't stand the thought of being around her after she got out of prison. I didn't blame him. We hadn't always felt this way. Before we moved to Hickory Ridge, my mother was serving a sentence of eleven months and twenty-nine days at a penal farm in Memphis. I remember the last visit we made to see her before my brothers and I moved to South Carolina. An officer patted her down in the prison's gym right in front of us. His hands moved from her denim work shirt to her jeans and rolled down to the soles of her bleached sneakers. She didn't flinch. She stood there and spread her arms apart as if she waited to be raised onto a cross.

I could tell by the look in Theo's eyes, the way his pupils twitched, that he couldn't take it. A part of him wanted to hurt the officer. But our mother passed through the inspection quickly, and when she sat with us, I placed my hand on Theo's shaking knee. When we finally started talking, all our mother could think about was getting out. She wanted us to tell her if she looked ready to come back into the real world. Did she look good enough to be seen by her old friends? Was she fat? I didn't know what to say. "Of course you're not," or, "You look fine as you want to be." The idea of my mother getting out was frightening, for me at least. I wasn't ready for the drinking to start up again, the screaming, the sudden outbursts of rage she experienced if the house wasn't clean, or if we were too quiet, or if she just felt the urge to get her hands on something, to twist or hit. Theo was the one to speak up. He held one of her hands and looked at her for a moment. I wonder if we saw the same woman. The woman who made us heart-shaped pancakes on Valentine's Day? The woman who once chased us with a baseball bat around the house when we were ten or eleven? The woman sitting in front of us then, who had been reduced to burning colored pencils for eyeliner? Maybe he didn't see any of those women. He just told her that she was beautiful and, honestly, shouldn't give a damn what people thought. And we didn't cry, just laughed at how silly we felt. All of us in that prison.

Getting Started with the "Write" Stuff: Time, Tools, and Turf

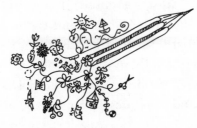

Soccer practice, emails and texts from friends, feeding the dog, cleaning your room ... not to mention the dreaded H-word: HOMEWORK! You are already sooooo busy—how could you ever squeeze in time for writing?

Not to mention, your computer is a piece of junk and you share a room with your sister/brother/pet cobra lunching on live mice. How are you supposed to create a brilliant piece of writing when you can't even hear yourself think half the time?

Does this sound familiar? Lots of writers know they want to write but mysteriously find themselves distracted. To get started, there are a few things you will want to set up to help you avoid getting sidetracked when you should be writing, also known as the "Three Ts": time, tools, and turf. The fact is, the hardest part of writing can be those first steps: making the time to do it, getting the writing materials you need ready to go, and finding a good place to write. Once you get over these first hurdles and actually start scribbling or typing real words, you are a writer.

Famous writers often have famous habits that help them write. Victor Hugo made his servant lock him in a room until he finished some writing. Ernest Hemingway marched upstairs every morning to his writing room, unlocking the door only to let in one of his six-toed cats!

You really won't have to lock yourself alone in a room to be a writer, but there are some things you can do that will make it easier for you to get started. If you're writing on your computer, turn off your email notifications. (Tip: No texting while you are writing!) In fact, try not to use the internet at all while you're writing. If you think of things to look up, keep a list to refer back to later so that you can stay focused. If you find your family distracting, try using earplugs to block out the noise of your house, or have an honest chat with your family about needing some quiet time. It might help to tell them that you plan to work for a specific amount of time—say, one hour—instead of just a general "can you be quiet forever" kind of request. You may be pleasantly surprised at how willing your family is to support you doing something as important as writing...if you just ask.

Once you have decided to start writing, tell yourself that no one needs to read what you write—the important thing is to get words on paper (or computer). It doesn't really matter what comes out—real writers admit that they write tons of junk, but that's where they find the good stuff that later turns out to be their best writing. Here are some suggestions to help you get started.

Finding the "Write" Time

Some writers like to set aside large chunks of time every day for their writing. Stephen King, for example, writes eight hours a day, every day of the year. The only days he takes off are his birthday, Christmas, and the Fourth of July!

But you don't *have* to give up your entire social life to be a writer. In fact, writing doesn't even have to take up large blocks of time, like school writing assignments can. When you get hungry for some food, you eat, right? And sometimes a little snack is the perfect thing. Well, when you get hungry to write, you should write! And it can be "snack" writing—a little bit here, a little bit there. Try scheduling a short, before-breakfast writing snack, limiting yourself to ten or twenty minutes. You could use a book of poetry (Robert Frost or Emily Dickinson work well) and respond to one line a day.

As you go through your day, when you see something or get an idea for writing, take a writing snack and jot yourself a quick note. Sometimes these are seeds that you can expand on later. Promise yourself to write something every day, every other day, or even just once a week—even if it's only a few lines. Pretty soon, your writing practices will get you in better shape as a writer, and your appetite for writing will grow. A little snack won't be enough anymore, and you'll find yourself stretching out your morning sessions or scheduling longer sessions just before bed or after basketball practice. Before you know it, you'll actually start looking forward to your writing sessions!

Collecting the "Write" Tools

One of the best things about writing is that you don't need a bunch of expensive gear to do it. Whether you're listing ideas in a journal or typing up that last chapter of your brilliant novel, you deserve to use tools that work for you. But that doesn't mean you have to have a whole new room, or a bunch of expensive supplies either. Your writing toolbox just needs to include things that help your writing.

Choosing something to write *in* is a good place to start. You might like a hardcover marble composition book because you can use it without a desk. Or you might prefer a spiral-bound notebook, with or without lines. Maybe you'd like to use a computer instead. Some authors, like fantasy novelist Peter V. Brett, have even typed entire books on their phones! If you prefer a journal, think about size: Does it need to be light, so you can carry it in your backpack, small to fit in your pocket, or will it stay at home on your desk? Do you like big fat pages where your thoughts can wander, or small pages that are easy to fill? (Tip: Sometimes a plain journal is easier to write in than a fancy one.) Do you like writing in pencil or ink? If you're using a computer, is it set up the way you want? Can you type comfortably? If you're writing your journal entries in a blog, experiment with blogging platforms until you learn what you prefer. Think about what makes you comfortable while writing, and choose your tools with those preferences in mind.

Famous Diarists

We have mentioned many, many times how important it is for a writer to keep a diary and never throw anything away. But don't take our word for it: here are some examples of famous writers who used their diaries as places to sort out creative problems.

- Twenty-six-year-old Kingsley Amis drafted poems in a notebook in 1948. Over the next year he revisited the writing on one page three times—once in disgust, then in relief, and finally in gratitude—adding dated diary entries each time. His first response to his writing was "it's not going to get better than this, it's going to get worse." Later he wrote of the same work: "Thank God I no longer feel like that." Finally he congratulated himself for having kept the writing and decided that it was worth it.
- When interviewed about his diaries, writer E. B. White called his entries "rubbish." Yet as a young boy of eight, he began to keep a diary. In his first draft of *The Trumpet of the Swan*, the young protagonist, Sam Beaver, takes out his diary—"just a cheap notebook that was always by his bed"—and confides an exciting secret: his discovery of a swan's nest. Sam (like the young White) ends his diary entries with a question to give himself something to ponder as he drifts off to sleep.

- When author John Steinbeck set out to write *The Grapes of Wrath*, he did so with the help of a diary. The first entry in the diary was: "Here is the diary of a book and it will be interesting to see how it works out." Steinbeck used the diary to keep track of his progress as he began a new novel about American migrant workers in 1938. He depended on it as a tool to jump-start each writing day. Fighting debilitating self-doubt and everyday distractions, he pressed on toward his goal, invigorated by his theme. "I grew again to love the story," he wrote after getting through a difficult stretch, "to love and admire the people who are so much stronger and purer and braver than I am."

Creating the "Write" Turf

Next, think about *where* you like to write. At a desk? Lying on the floor? In your favorite chair? At your local coffee shop? No matter where, you should find a spot that's open and inviting for you, and where all of your writing tools are easily available. Keep your writing turf clear and clean so picking up junk won't sidetrack you when you're ready to write. You deserve a space of your own that is so encouraging you'll smile when you see it and *want* to get started.

If you choose to make your turf in a permanent space, be creative. Why not decorate? Plenty of writers put up inspiring quotes, pictures, posters, and so on in their writing spaces to help keep their creativity going. Decorating is a way to mark your writing turf clearly, for all to see. When you are sitting there, you'll be sending the signal "Writer at Work!"—to yourself and to your family. It's not hard to make your writing space happen; just make sure that all of the following items are there waiting for you in your special place:

Writing Stuff Checklist:

_____ favorite pens/pencils

_____ favorite paper/journal/notebook/typewriter/computer

_____ glue stick (not necessary, but great for pasting important tidbits into your journal)

_____ file folders (not necessary, but handy for keeping your different writing projects organized)

_____ headphones/earmuffs/earplugs (not necessary, but nice for tuning out the phone or your noisy family)

_____ flash drive or other storage device if you're using a computer (don't forget to back up your files!)

_____ box or drawer for stashing everything

Tips for Collecting the "Write" Ideas

Journaling

Who needs a journal? You do! If you plan to write and sound real (or even *un*real), there is no greater source for ideas and words than real life. It's important to keep a journal and to write in it every day. What you write does not have to make sense or be perfect—just try to record what you notice. Each time you look through your journal, you won't believe how many ideas and words and phrases you can use from it.

Some writers use journals as diaries and record their daily activities and thoughts in them. This can be a great way for you to start thinking about your world and making sense of it. A diary journal can be a great best friend, always ready to listen, always forgiving, never judgmental. If you like this idea, you might want to give your journal a name, like Anne Frank did. At first, Anne just listed the day's activities in her new diary. But after she named the diary "Kitty," she began writing in it as if she were writing to a person. The diary became a true friend with whom Anne could share her hopes, fears, and dreams. And, as you probably know already, that diary also became one of the most powerful books ever written.

Your journal can be a traditional paper notebook, a file on your computer, or even a blog. If you like to use your blog as a writing journal, remember that you don't have to share your writing with the world until you're ready! Every blog platform has privacy settings, so think about how much of yourself you want to expose and set them accordingly.

You don't always have to just *write* in a journal—you can sketch and draw, or even use scrapbook techniques. Writers often use journals as memory joggers, so keep a glue stick handy and paste in movie stubs, photos from magazines, great newspaper headlines, anything that strikes you. If you contribute to it every day, pretty soon you'll find yourself looking back over your entries and discovering a goldmine of ideas and language to use in your writing.

Observing

Writers have lots of different ways they keep journals. Some write long, rambling paragraphs, some list short thoughts, some copy down words or phrases they overhear. Good writers make readers feel as if they are on the scene, observing and becoming part of the story. Good writers must learn to observe and write about what they see, hear, and feel. Hang around, listen, pay attention—and be sure to write it all down. You *think* you'll remember the comment that jerk made in the cafeteria, but you won't when you need it for a villain's remark in your next story!

You can actually go on little "spy trips" with your journal, observing your world and writing down what you see. Look at what's in front of you as if it were a scene in a movie; keep an eye peeled for interesting characters, and write how they act and move, as well as what they say. Write down how the sky looks or how the air smells in that particular setting. Jot down scraps of conversation—nothing is more real than reality. Only you can know the best spots for spy trips in your area, but here are some good general places for observing human behavior: a crowded park, the school cafeteria, a city bus or subway, the local mall…hey, your very own kitchen at dinnertime is the perfect place to watch a "normal" family in action!

Reading!

It's probably not going to come as a big surprise, but almost all great writers love to read! That's often how they got interested in writing in the first place. And it's not unusual for a writer of one kind of book (say, sci-fi) to prefer reading completely different kinds of books (say, poetry). The point is that any reading is a huge resource for you as a writer. Reading will help you find words, phrases, topics, characters, and styles for your own writing.

Archetypes: Haven't I Heard That Story Somewhere Before?

Since the dawn of time, when humans first began telling stories in caves, the same types of plots and characters have appeared over and over again. The more you read, the more you'll notice how authors reuse these same models, or archetypes.

There is the archetypal hero (Bilbo Baggins, Luke Skywalker, Alice in Wonderland, Meg from *A Wrinkle in Time*, Harry Potter), a lonely character who doesn't think he or she is good enough to be a hero. In the archetypal hero story, the hero leaves on a perilous journey, meets some buddies to help in the adventure, and finally triumphs in the end using his or her courage and cleverness.

Fairy tales are full of archetypal characters: the innocent victim (Snow White, Cinderella, Little Red Riding Hood) who is preyed on by a villain (wicked stepmothers, evil sorcerers, hungry old ladies living in candy houses) and rescued in the end by the good guy/gal (handsome prince, fairy godmother, brave woodsman).

There are lots of interesting character archetypes and story archetypes repeated in great literature. Watch out for them in your reading, and then you can decide which pieces of these tried-and-true models you might want to use in your writing.

Reading is also a great way to check out the competition. In most jobs, people have to research what others in their field are doing. No problem for writers—all you have to do is read to find out what other writers are up to. Once you start writing in your journal and taking yourself seriously as a writer, you will find yourself reading with new eyes. You'll start to notice how other writers deal with things you're wondering about, such as character development, setting description, or use of metaphor.

Young Author Profile:
Reeves Wiedeman

Twenty-five-year-old **Reeves Wiedeman** graduated from Boston College and now works as a fact-checker at *The New Yorker*.

When did you know you wanted to be a writer?
I originally wanted to be a journalist. I wrote for my high school newspaper, then my college newspaper, all with the intent of one day being a newspaper reporter. It wasn't until senior year

of college that I began to see myself as a writer. I took several courses in creative nonfiction and started reading magazines with more literary content—*The Atlantic*, *Esquire*, *The New Yorker*—and though I continued writing newspaper stories, they started to become longer features like the ones I was reading.

What do you like to write the most and why?

I do all nonfiction, or that's all I do with any success. Poetry has never been my cup of tea—as a writer or reader—and I've never had the imagination for fiction. That said, I've started a number of short stories and screenplays over the years to see if I can make one work. It's useful to write in different styles, to take lessons from my attempts at fiction and use them in my nonfiction.

What are your goals for your writing future?

They change all the time, in part due to my interests, in part due to changes in the industry. The first goal, I suppose, is to simply make a living off of writing alone. Then, in an ideal world, I'd love to be writing magazine stories of all kinds: long profiles, short humorous pieces, and everything in between.

What was your first published piece (and format) and how did you feel?

On an amateur level, it was for my high school newspaper. I don't remember what the article was or how I felt, but I will say this: if you want to be a writer, and you're not writing for your high school or college newspaper, then you're wasting an excellent opportunity. Even if your interest is in fiction, student papers offer a chance to (a) write, (b) learn the value of research, (c) get edited, and (d) get published. My first professional publication was in the *Boston Globe*. It was a story I wrote for a creative non-fiction class, about a college classmate of mine who was blind but still managed to play in the marching band. It showed me that the barrier to entry at professional publications isn't all that high; you just need to present them with a story they can't turn down.

20

Where else have you been published?

Since then, I've written for all types of publications—*The New Yorker*, *New York Times*, political websites, sports publications, local newspapers. As a young writer, you should be looking as widely as possible for places to publish stories.

Do you write full-time, and, if not, would you like to? What would be your dream job?

I don't write full-time but that's the goal. My ideal job, as of now, is to be a staff writer at a magazine.

What advice would you give to a young writer?

Being a good writer is not enough. Starting out in the journalism world, you have to spend as much time as you can pitching stories, meeting with people, and failing. You don't need a connection to do this: go to your college alumni database, find all the journalists, and see if they'll have coffee with you. They might not give you a job right now, but two years later—as happened to me once—they might come back, looking for you to write a story.

Do you think reading helps your writing?

Of course. The beauty of being a writer is that reading is part of your job. Read as widely as possible: if you want to write fiction, read newspapers, and vice versa.

What are your favorite reads?

I'm a magazine junkie. *The New Yorker* is a must, and good reads can be found in *Harper's*, *Esquire*, *New York*, and *Wired*, among many others.

Name some of the authors who have inspired you and why.

Most are at *The New Yorker*: John McPhee, Tad Friend, Nick Paumgarten, and Anthony Lane have all significantly influenced the way I write, even if I don't always show it.

If you know what type of writing you want to do (poetry, horror, and so on), reading that kind of book or article or blog will really help you get started. No one is expected to learn a craft without first seeing samples of the finished product. How could a boat builder construct a sailboat if she had never even seen one before? So, consider reading part of a writer's job—part of *your* job—and one of the best parts!

Reading is especially good to do when you're stuck in your writing. A really good book will take you on a little vacation to other worlds that renew your creativity and excitement about writing. Giving your brain a vacation by reading is often just what you need to get started writing again.

Book Clubs

Believe it or not, there are lots of other kids out there who love to read, and they are a fantastic resource for you as a writer. Joining a book club will introduce you to new books, friends who share your passion, and tons of great writing ideas—not just from the books, but from the club members as well. Ask a librarian at school or at your local library for clubs in your area. When you find one, check out the list of books they've read in the past few meetings to see if they interest you. This is a good way to see if that club's reading choices will fit with yours.

Book clubs not only open you up to new kinds of writing and authors, but they are also your golden opportunity to see how readers react to different kinds of writing and to find out what they like and don't like about various stories, styles, and techniques. Someday people will be reading your writing, and your book-club experiences will remind you to keep your future audience in mind when you write.

If you can't find a book club, just start your own—all it takes is one other person! Here's how they work:

1. Agree on a regular meeting place, day, and time (like the first Wednesday of the month at 4:30 PM at the local library or at the house of whichever member chose that month's book).

2. Agree to read that month's selected book, which is chosen by one club member, perhaps with advice from a librarian.
3. Discuss any ground rules, like maximum number of pages a chosen book can be or that the book must be available in paperback or obtainable from local libraries.
4. For each meeting, the person who chose that month's book should bring a few questions to discuss about the book and/ or author. Take turns being the book chooser.
5. Food is optional but a definite plus! Many groups take turns hosting, or sometimes all bring a snack or refreshment to share.
6. If you have a friend who can't make it to the meeting, try using an online conferencing service (like Skype) to include him or her in the discussion! Or if you have lots of friends in other cities, you can chat online with everyone to conduct your meeting. Some popular book clubs meet entirely online. The science fiction blog io9, for example, selects a book each month for its fans to read. Then they have a discussion about it in the blog's comment section. Sometimes the book's author even joins the conversation! You can also join or create an online book club (check out sites like Goodreads). Just remember to be safe: Don't give out your personal details in online discussions, and don't agree to meet up with anyone you don't already know in real life.

Now You're Good to Go!

Getting started as a writer means making the time, creating the space, and having the tools ready. One author writes in the middle of a cornfield, in a little white cottage that her husband built just for her to write in. Another writer uses the kitchen table when no one else is home and works only on Sunday afternoons. One novelist had a full-time job as an elevator operator and took her writing snacks on the subway to and from work every day. Like these writers, you will discover what works best for you. Finding the "write" time, tools, and turf will help your creativity blossom and is the first step to becoming a real writer!

How One Author Finds
the "Write" Stuff

Todd Strasser—author of more than 150 books, including *The Wave* and the Help! I'm Trapped series, as well as movie scripts and magazine articles—has some definite opinions about the "write" time, tools, and turf that work for him.

Where do you write?
I write in a room with lots of windows so I can look outside and see the world (well, at least a backyard and some squirrels).

How do you find time for your writing?
Good question. I get frustrated by how much time I waste doing busywork. Someone once wrote, "I love writing, it's the paperwork I can't stand." I thought they were kidding. My current schedule is to write from around 8 AM until somewhere between noon and 2 PM. After that it's time for letters, emails, speaking arrangements, etc. Sometimes I get another writing session in during the late afternoon.

What do you write with?
I do as much work as possible on the keyboard. My handwriting is horrible and I often cannot figure out what I wrote. So except for quick notes here and there that will soon be added to the text, I let my fingers do the talking.

Does reading help you as a writer?
Since somewhere between 75 and 90 percent of writing is rewriting, reading is essential. After all, isn't rewriting the process of trying to improve what you've written? How can one know how to improve one's writing without reading what others have written? Reading is probably the only way the writer can learn what "good" writing is, and then apply it to his or her own writing.

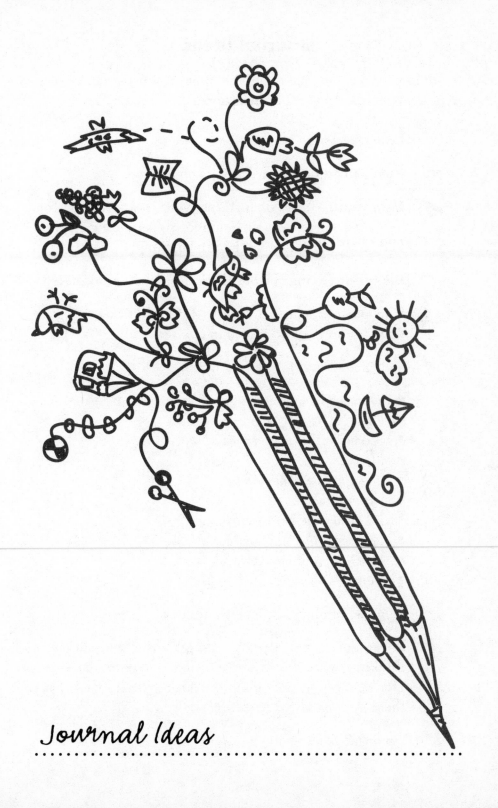

Journal Ideas

Journal Ideas

Cut this page out and glue it into the front of your journal or keep it next to your computer for inspiration.

 Daily events

 Your daily thoughts, reactions, and feelings

 Lists: your favorites of anything, your least favorites, Top Ten lists, current movies, music, singers, songs, sports stars, cool words, quotes, books, anything!

 Weird/interesting cut-outs: articles, photos, headlines

 Random mementos: a movie or concert ticket, a leaf, a flower, a note passed to you in class

 Sentence starters for journal writing:

- *This reminded me of...*
- *I wish...*
- *Speaking as so-and-so, I would say...*
- *I wonder...*
- *If that happened to me...*
- *I would change...*
- *If I could do it over again, I would...*
- *I can't imagine...*
- *What surprised me was...*
- *At first, I thought..., but then...*

 Reviews of movies, concerts, or books

 Stream of consciousness writing (Write without even thinking what words are pouring out onto the page. Don't stop for five minutes. Then check out what's there. Any patterns? Anything cool?)

 "Spy trip" field notes

Young Author Profile:
Alina Mahvish Din

When she was just eleven years old, **Alina Mahvish Din** won second place in the Roald Dahl Essay Contest. Inspired by this win, she submitted other work as well. A short article about Ramadan (a holy Islamic holiday) was published in a homeschooling journal, as was an essay she submitted to the book *Girls Who Rocked the World 2*.

Why do you love to write?
It's easier for me to get my feelings out on paper rather than saying them out loud. When I finish writing something, I feel a great sense of accomplishment, and a lasting feeling of self-respect is left within me. I try to make whatever I write come from my heart, be it a book report, essay, or a journal entry.

How do you come up with topics?
When you aren't given a specific topic and you don't know what to write about, don't stress! It's often helpful to write about something you know a lot about or something you like very much. Write about your favorite movie or role model, the way your best friend makes you smile, the smell of brownies, or a new law that ought to be made. Write about a picture that puts a smile (or a frown) on your face, or about the best present you ever received. Think! Get deep into your head! As Alfred Hitchcock said, "Ideas come from everywhere."

What are some cool ideas for getting started with writing?
Write a letter to the editor of a magazine telling them why you liked or disliked an article they published. Send email and letters

to your friends and family. Join your school's newspaper staff; if your school doesn't have a newspaper, start one! Create a website dedicated to your passion, or find some that you like and post your opinions on stuff from politics to pop stars. Keep a journal and write in it whenever your heart desires. Start a scrapbook with words and pictures that describe your everyday life.

Which author has inspired and improved your own writing?

I admire the way Gail Carson Levine writes. Her books are funny, interesting, and beautiful. Publishing companies wouldn't accept her work for a *long* time, but she never gave up. She stuck with her dream and kept writing because she knew that was what she loved to do. Sometimes I feel hopeless when it comes to writing something particular, and I wonder if I'll be able to get my feelings across. When I think of Mrs. Levine, it helps to know that even an extraordinary writer like her had discouraging moments.

What advice do you have for other young writers?

My advice to aspiring writers is to write! Write, write, write. Enter writing contests; send your work to publishing companies, magazines, and newspapers. If you don't feel like sharing your work with others, just keep a book of your work for yourself. Follow your dream, whether you're a poet, playwright, lyricist, novelist, journalist, or whatever! Write in any way you feel comfortable. Save ALL of what you've written, because, believe me, you'll be glad you did! Become pen pals with your favorite writers, asking them for advice. Never give up your dream, and don't stop writing!

Poetry, Fiction, Sci-Fi, and More: Exploring the Different Genres

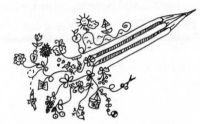

*I*t was a dark and stormy night . . ." No, no, no. How about "The spaceship slowly lifted out of Mars's atmosphere . . ." or "I was ten years old and living on the waterfront when my countrymen decided to dump Britain's tea into the Boston Harbor and start a war . . ."

The ideas swirl inside your head, but you just can't decide what kind of story to write. You thought of a great sci-fi plot in the shower this morning . . . but maybe there's a brilliant poet inside you dying to get out . . . but newspaper reporting has always seemed appealing. Ahhhh!

There are so many directions you can go, so many different kinds of writing—called *genres*—for you to investigate. How about science fiction or historical fiction? Or are you a mystery fan? You might prefer nonfiction, covering sports for your school paper. Have you ever considered writing a play or some poetry?

Quiz: What's Your Genre?

Take this completely unscientific quiz to see which genre you might want to explore.

1. At parties, I like to . . .

   a. talk intensely about a current event in the news to find out what other people know.

   b. people watch. It's fun to see how the popular kids act and figure out who is the rebel in the crowd. People are *so* fascinating!

   c. observe the drama between my friends, what they are saying to each other and how they are saying it.

   d. get lost in the sound of many people talking at once. I can pick out words here and there and make a collage of them in my head. The words don't make a lot of sense, but the weird combination fascinates me.

   e. wonder if the people around me just look human but are really alien spies!

2. My imaginary friend is . . .

   a. a kid detective.

   b. an encyclopedia with two legs and two arms.

   c. a cat in a hat whose name is Pat.

   d. You're kidding, right? Who needs an imaginary friend?

   e. Chewie from *Star Wars*.

3. If I got a $20 gift certificate to a bookstore, I'd race out and buy . . .

   a. the newest book by Stephen King. I've already read all his earlier stuff.

   b. Alicia Keys's poetry book *Tears for Water*.

   c. a copy of *The Catcher in the Rye* or a book about the making of *Inception*.

   d. *Persepolis* or a biography of my favorite hero.

   e. *The Outsiders* by S. E. Hinton or *Switched* by Amanda Hocking.

4. My philosophy is . . .

   a. "Don't let the truth get in the way of a good story."

   b. "May the Force be with you."

c. "Poetry is the eloquence of truth."

d. "All the world's a stage."

e. "Truth is stranger than fiction."

5. At the state fair, I would spend most of my time . . .

a. riding the Starship 4000. It feels like you're in outer space on that thing.

b. learning about all the different animals on display.

c. eavesdropping on kids in the snow-cone line.

d. on the Ferris wheel. I love watching the colors of the sunset and feeling the wind in my hair from up there.

e. watching the various performers onstage.

6. My favorite thing about writing is . . .

a. interviewing people and asking hard questions about important issues.

b. getting my innermost thoughts across in the fewest, most beautiful words.

c. imagining fantastic creatures and faraway lands.

d. creating interesting characters that feel real.

e. imagining how people will become my characters on stage and how the audience will react to my words.

7. When I daydream in class, I . . .

a. imagine myself as a reporter, traveling in a foreign country to cover a world-changing news event.

b. create haikus from snippets of what the teacher is saying.

c. imagine that the teacher is actually a giant man-eating insect that can disguise itself as a human during certain phases of its life.

d. put the whole class in a movie and think up tons of exciting plot twists that could happen.

e. think about all the stories I could write on the subject being discussed.

8. My idea of a great weekend afternoon is . . .

a. visiting a local garden and writing a long poem about a just-blooming rose bush.

b. going to a triple-header movie marathon. Who cares if it's sunny outside?

c. sitting at a café downtown with my laptop, watching people go by and living their lives, while I write it all down for story material.

d. coming across a reporter filming a news story. Maybe she'll interview me and I can speak my mind on the issue.

e. playing a complex fantasy game with my friends, where we each get to play different wizards.

9. My favorite game to play is . . .

a. Bananagrams.

b. Life.

c. charades.

d. Cranium.

e. *The Sims.*

10. When a teacher calls on me and I don't know the answer, I . . .

a. create an elaborate story that *sounds* like it might be an answer but is mostly just my imagination.

b. tell him that my pet dragon burned up my homework.

c. tell him the truth: Sorry, but I don't know the answer.

d. put my hand on my forehead and sigh dramatically (my sickness act always works).

e. tell him that all answers are debatable anyway.

Scoring:

Add up your points for each answer you circled. Check out the meaning of your total below.

1. a) 1   b) 3   c) 2   d) 5   e) 4
2. a) 4   b) 1   c) 5   d) 3   e) 2

3. a) 4   b) 5   c) 2   d) 1   e) 3
4. a) 3   b) 4   c) 5   d) 2   e) 1
5. a) 4   b) 1   c) 3   d) 5   e) 2
6. a) 1   b) 5   c) 4   d) 3   e) 2
7. a) 1   b) 5   c) 4   d) 2   e) 3
8. a) 5   b) 2   c) 3   d) 1   e) 4
9. a) 5   b) 3   c) 2   d) 1   e) 4
10. a) 3   b) 4   c) 1   d) 2   e) 5

Key to the categories:

10–17 points:
You are intrigued by real life and history. Read about current events from as many different sources as you can and get to know more about journalism and nonfiction writing.

18–25 points:
You love drama! You'll probably enjoy playwriting and screen-writing. Get involved in your school's drama scene and keep your eyes open for local workshops for beginning screenwriters or playwrights.

26–33 points:
You have a talent for observing your world and developing what you see into stories. You'd be great at writing fiction.

34–41 points:
You read each *Harry Potter* in one sitting, think J. R. R. Tolkien is a genius, and wish Stephen King would run for president. You are a sci-fi/fantasy/mystery nut.

42–50 points:
To you, all the world is a poem. Feed your soul and go check out a book of poetry and a few poetry websites.

Now that you have a tiny idea of which genres you might be interested in, here are some descriptions to whet your appetite.

Fiction

You like to watch and observe, learn about people and relationships, share your ideas, and take your readers on adventures.

Fiction writing isn't real life, but feels like it is. Fiction stories are completely made up but are often based on real-life experiences that the author had, watched others have, or heard about.

Good fiction has characters you feel like you're getting to know, places that you feel like you've visited, and plot events that keep you turning the pages. Fiction writers are excellent observers and listeners, often spying on strangers, jotting notes that seem to have no meaning at the time, and saving material that helps them remember the specifics of settings. They like to learn about their made-up people and settings, and enjoy reading and listening to information on their topics. Mystery, science fiction, fantasy, horror, and historical fiction are examples of some different kinds of fiction genres you may want to check out.

Mystery

Does Nancy Drew ring a bell? How about the Hardy Boys? If you like mystery, you like stories or novels with plots where you need to put together the pieces of the puzzle to figure out who killed the chauffeur.

One of the best mystery writers of all time is Agatha Christie, and you'd learn a lot about how to write a suspenseful story by reading some of her books—*Murder on the Orient Express*, *Death on the Nile*, or *And Then There Were None* to name a few. She also wrote mystery plays, including *The Mousetrap*, which is the longest-running play in history.

Here are some current popular mystery writers and titles to get to know:

Faces of the Gone by Brad Parks
The Bone Chamber by Robin Burcell
The Girl with the Dragon Tattoo by Stieg Larsson
The Sweetness at the Bottom of the Pie by Alan Bradley

> *A Trace of Smoke* by Rebecca Cantrell
> *What the Night Knows* by Dean Koontz
> *The Hanging Tree* by Bryan Gruley

Science Fiction & Fantasy

These two genres have many similarities. Both have some element of the unexplained. It might be a story about a time traveler, like Madeleine L'Engle's *A Wrinkle in Time*; a story with a paranormal twist, like the Wicked Lovely series by Melissa Marr; or a story set in a dystopian world, like Lois Lowry's *The Giver*. Both types of stories can be totally made up or can include real people as characters. Stories are considered *high fantasy* when the action takes place entirely in a different realm. And some people are surprised to find out that books like *Charlotte's Web* are technically fantasy (after all, pigs don't talk!). If you think you might want to write sci-fi or fantasy stories, get inspired by reading a few of the masters:

> The Lord of the Rings trilogy by J. R. R. Tolkien
> *The Golden Compass* by Philip Pullman
> Earthsea Cycle series by Ursula K. Le Guin
> *The Book of Three* by Lloyd Alexander
> *Uglies* by Scott Westerfeld
> *The Giver* by Lois Lowry
> The Chronicles of Narnia series by C. S. Lewis
> The Harry Potter series by J. K. Rowling
> The Twilight Saga by Stephenie Meyer
> The Hunger Games trilogy by Suzanne Collins

Horror

When someone says "horror," who doesn't think of Stephen King? A story fits the horror genre if it gives you the heebie-jeebies, makes your heart pound, keeps you up all night—you get the idea. Like sci-fi and fantasy, horror often incorporates unknown elements. But unlike those genres, horror usually takes place in the real world—the real world gone horribly wrong. Here are some scary books that should have you quaking under your covers:

Frankenstein by Mary Shelley
Dracula by Bram Stoker
The Vampire Chronicles by Anne Rice
Almost *anything* by Stephen King
In the Forests of the Night by Amelia Atwater-Rhodes
Don't Look Behind You by Lois Duncan
It's the First Day of School . . . Forever! by R. L. Stine
The Forest of Hands and Teeth by Carrie Ryan
Rot & Ruin by Jonathan Maberry

> *Don't be afraid to try your hand at crossing genres. You have an idea for a dystopian mystery? A romantic horror set in the middle ages? Give it a try! Write the story that feels right to you.*

Historical Fiction

This genre is just what it sounds like: a *made up* story set in the *real* past. *Catherine, Called Birdy* by Karen Cushman is a perfect example of how to write in this genre. You might also enjoy these other historical novels:

Ruby in the Smoke by Philip Pullman
The Book Thief by Markus Zusak
Frenchman's Creek by Daphne du Maurier
Between Shades of Gray by Ruta Sepetys
The Once and Future King by T. H. White
The True Confessions of Charlotte Doyle by Avi
Annexed by Sharon Dogar
Lyddie by Katherine Paterson
Chains by Laurie Halse Anderson

Realistic Fiction

This is a type of fiction that places emphasis on the truthful representation of the actual. That is, it deals with situations or events in a way that you might handle them in your own life. Here are some examples:

The Absolutely True Diary of a Part-Time Indian by Sherman Alexie
Staying Fat for Sarah Byrnes by Chris Crutcher
Just Listen by Sarah Dessen
The View from Saturday by E. L. Konigsburg
Are You There God? It's Me, Margaret. by Judy Blume
Holes by Louis Sachar
To Kill a Mockingbird by Harper Lee
Thirteen Reasons Why by Jay Asher

Short Stories

Many of the authors we've already mentioned write in more than one genre. Many novelists, for example, also write short stories. Novels and short stories are similar in that they both have a beginning, middle, and end. But short stories are different because . . . well, they're *short*. That is, they are often set in a smaller time period, like one afternoon, or revolve around one particular event, instead of having a long plot with many events. Short stories have to say a lot in less space—which is not as easy as it sounds. There are a million good short stories, but here are some of our favorite short-story writers:

John Cheever
Chris Crutcher
Cynthia Rylant
Katherine Mansfield
Peter Dickinson
Eudora Welty
Alice Munro
Gish Jen
Shirley Jackson

Poetry

Lots of authors experiment with poetry when they first begin writing. Poets can still tell a story, but they tend to experiment more with images, rhyme, the way words and phrases *sound*, how they make you *feel*—even how they *look* on the page. Here's just a sampling of some of the fabulous poets you really should meet, especially if you think this is your genre:

Emily Dickinson
Maya Angelou
Mary Oliver
E. E. Cummings
Robert Frost
Langston Hughes
Elizabeth Bishop
Shel Silverstein
Dr. Seuss

> *Each genre has its own rules and conventions. Learn the rules of your genre so readers will know you're an expert in your field, but be careful to not let your writing become formulaic. Experiment to figure out when to break the rules and when to uphold them.*

Plays & Screenplays

A play is written to be performed by actors on a stage in front of a live audience. A screenplay is also written for actors but is meant to be recorded and made into a film or video. The more you know about how a live production works, both on and offstage, the easier it will be for you to write these genres. Getting involved in school plays or a local theater is a great way to learn (see chapter 10 about writing careers), but reading these famous playwrights will also help:

A Raisin in the Sun by Lorraine Hansberry
Romeo and Juliet or *A Midsummer Night's Dream*
　　are good Shakespeare plays to start with

A Streetcar Named Desire by Tennessee Williams
The Crucible by Arthur Miller
Our Town by Thornton Wilder
Pygmalion by George Bernard Shaw

How One Author Chose Her Genre

Wendelin Van Draanen is the 1999 winner for the Edgar Award for Best Juvenile mystery. Her book *Sammy Keyes and the Hotel Thief* was her first children's mystery. There are now twelve Sammy Keyes novels with the goal to complete the series with the twentieth title.

How did you decide to write children's mysteries?

I have always loved mysteries and, in fact, have written a couple of unpublished adult mysteries. I sent sample chapters of one of these to my editor and asked if she knew anyone I might send them to. She didn't, but said if I ever wanted to try a mystery for middle-grade readers to send it to her. There was this big click in my brain and I thought, *Yes, of course!* So I tried my hand with Sammy Keyes and wrote the first four at one time.

What experiences help you to create your characters?

Until recently, I worked as a computer science teacher. Being the computer teacher, I wound up with . . . well, let's put it this way: the popular kids don't join the computer club or the chess club. So my room became the place where the sort of outcasts would come and feel at home, and I think that all comes into play when I develop the characters in my mysteries. Watching and listening to what is around you is so important. And I remember what it was like to not be very comfortable with other kids—I guess most of us go through a phase like that. When I write I just kind of fall back on being in seventh grade again.

What do you hope readers get from your mysteries?
I hope readers can identify with Sammy to the point that they feel they can learn something from her without feeling like she is giving them a lecture. Making Sammy a believable character is just as important to me as making her a super sleuth.

Nonfiction

You love to learn new things, gather information, read and write about real things, and share knowledge and news with others.

Nonfiction writing is all true. It could be a life story (an autobiography or short memoir about your life, or a biography about someone else's life) or a true story about a historical event, like the search for King Tut's tomb. It could also be a fact-based opinion piece, like an essay on school dress codes or a review of a school play or rock concert.

Nonfiction writers like reading about their subjects and getting lots of facts and juicy details to support their ideas. They do their research everywhere, often interviewing their subjects and then publishing those interviews. They visit websites, use libraries, and scope out museums when researching their ideas. There are many kinds of nonfiction writing, but essays, journalism, historical nonfiction, biography, and autobiography are a few of the most common types.

Essays

You can write an essay about almost anything—your opinion on a recent event at school, your feelings about peanut butter and jelly sandwiches, or your views on something in the news. Here are some great essayists and/or essays to check out:

E. B. White (yup, the same guy who wrote *Stuart Little* and *Charlotte's Web*)
Up in the Old Hotel by Joseph Mitchell

Journalism

Journalists cover the events of everyday life in magazines, on the radio, in newspapers, and on TV. If you are interested in news, join your school newspaper and start writing about school news events. Or you can start a blog about topics that interest you. But don't be afraid to think even bigger—you could offer to cover teen news for your local paper too. To find out more about journalism, here are a few helpful books:

America's Best Newspaper Writing: A Collection of ASNE Prizewinners edited by Roy Peter Clark and Christopher Scanlan

Associated Press Broadcast News Handbook by Brad Kalbfeld

The Best American Sports Writing series edited by Peter Gammons (updated volumes released yearly)

The Camera Never Blinks: Adventures of a TV Journalist by Dan Rather

Journalistas: 100 Years of the Best Writing and Reporting by Women Journalists edited by Eleanor Mills

Heat and Light: Advice for the Next Generation of Journalists by Mike Wallace and Beth Knobel

Vicki Leonard, TV Writer

When did you know you wanted to be a writer?

I have written my whole life. When I was about eight, I discovered TV news. My uncle worked for CBS in documentaries and would bring home scripts. I'd watch the documentary with the script in hand. From that time on, I knew I would work in television.

What was your first job and how did you get started?

When I graduated from college, we were heading into an election year. I researched how the different news agencies covered elections and then set my sights on ABC News. I sent the head of the Special Events Unit a book outlining what I would write for background for reporters to use when they went on interviews. I got the job immediately! Always take the time to research companies and publications you are interested in. The more you know about them, the better you can sell your ideas!

How have your goals for your writing changed?

I got my first job in television when I was twenty-four. I was hired as a researcher for ABC News. It was an election year, so I covered the presidential campaign. I wrote all the candidate research for the reporters in the field. Soon I was on the road as a producer and writer. I loved my job: I met four presidents and countless other newsworthy people. I covered everything from the space shuttle to Prince Charles's wedding to Princess Diana. I decided that I wanted to explore other kinds of writing. In television, you always write to time. That is, if you have a piece of video that needs to be one minute and fifty seconds, that is all the time you have to tell a story. I wanted to work in print for a change and perhaps start my own publication. I did!

What was your first published piece (and format) and how did you feel?

The first piece I ever wrote was for my college newspaper. My high school did not have a paper or I would have started earlier. I wrote about friendship and how friends come in different packages. My best friend at the time was my eighty-two-year-old grandmother who gave me my passion for exploring the world of nonfiction. There is nothing like seeing your own byline.

What advice would you give to a young writer?

I think being a good writer is being a good listener and a good watcher. Know about the world around you. Follow writers you admire. I have some newspaper writers who I read regularly and they have blogs that I follow as well. Always make time to write and don't be afraid to try your hand at lots of kinds of writing. If you are interested in reporting for TV or print, read as many different sources as you can. I read five newspapers and check out the news on numerous different websites daily.

Do you think reading helps your writing?
Absolutely—you cannot be a good writer unless you read other people's writing! I read all kinds of writing: fiction, nonfiction, history, biography, essays . . . I never leave home without a book. I once got laughed at when a date discovered I had a book in my purse!

What are your favorite reads?
I read tons of magazines and love newspapers. One of my favorite authors, who I go back to time and again, is Ernie Pyle, an American journalist who wrote as a roving newspaper correspondent during World War II. Pyle had the ability to tell a story in a way that put you in his shoes. He caught the moment about which he was writing in a way few reporters before or since have been able to do.

Name some of the authors who have inspired you and why.
Ernie Pyle, Walter Cronkite, Charles Dickens, Henry James, J. K. Rowling, Edward R. Murrow, P. D. James, Ngaio Marsh. All of these writers inspire me because of the beautiful way they use language to change mere words into visions that I will keep with me always.

Historical Nonfiction

If you are fascinated by history, find a topic that intrigues you and start digging. Many historical nonfiction pieces start out as magazine or newspaper articles that writers wanted to expand on. Making an article into a full-length book gives an author the chance to include a lot more detail and information for the reader.

Here are some exciting examples of this genre:

The Perfect Storm by Sebastian Junger
In the Heart of the Sea by Nathaniel Philbrick
The Circus Fire by Stewart O'Nan
The Devil in the White City by Erik Larson
The Mapmaker's Wife by Robert Whitaker

Find a review site in your genre and volunteer to write reviews. Often, you get free books and bylines by offering to be a reader—most reviews on sites aren't paid, but you'll see what's new in you genre, get experience, and find other writers in the same boat as you.

Biography & Autobiography

A biography is the story of a person's life that is written by someone else. An autobiography is the story of a person's life that is written by that person. Both of these genres can be fascinating. Here are some old classics and some newer examples of these two genres:

Cleopatra: A Life by Stacy Schiff (biography)
Anne Frank: The Diary of a Young Girl by Anne Frank (autobiography)
I Know Why the Caged Bird Sings by Maya Angelou (autobiography)
Lincoln: A Photobiography and *Eleanor Roosevelt: A Life of Discovery* by Russell Freedman (biographies)

Exploring different genres is a first step for all writers. Don't be afraid to experiment. You may think you only like to write poetry...until you try playwriting. Or you may only enjoy writing fiction until you come across an event or a person in history that sparks your curiosity.

The Pulitzer Prize–winning author August Wilson, whose plays include *Fences* and *Ma Rainey's Black Bottom*, first wrote poetry. Stewart O'Nan had always written fiction until he heard about a horrible circus fire in 1944. The more he researched the tragic event, the more he felt he had to write the story as it actually happened. *The Circus Fire* was his first work of nonfiction. Truman Capote is equally famous for his fiction work *Breakfast at Tiffany's* and his groundbreaking account of a true crime described in his book *In Cold Blood*.

The very best way to pick your genre is to read examples of that genre. Try some of the books we listed, and then just go to the sections in the library. You'll soon discover which type of writing really grabs you, and you'll have a better idea of what you might want to write about.

Felice Kuan, Lyricist

When did you know you wanted to be a lyricist/ songwriter?
Ever since fourth grade, I knew that I wanted to write, but I thought writing was something people should do on the side, next to their "real" job. So I studied math in college and I became a math teacher for several years. I liked teaching, and I thought I would have plenty of time to write every day after school. How do you think that worked out? Terribly! It takes a lot of work to be a good teacher, and I spent hardly any time writing. So finally I promised myself I was going to make writing my real job instead. I quit teaching and went into graduate school for songwriting at New York University. Maybe one day I'll go back to teaching, but for now, I'm very happy writing!

What does a lyricist/songwriter do?
I write songs for musical theater shows. Usually I write the lyrics (words) and a partner or friend writes the music, but sometimes I compose the music too. I also write the dialogue and the plot of the musical. One of the most interesting things about writing

lyrics in musical theater is capturing the way different characters talk when they are singing. For example, Red Riding Hood is carefree and sweet, but she's also pretty dumb—so she might use simple words that are full of emotion, and she might repeat her words a few times. Meanwhile the deceptive and charming Wolf might use sophisticated vocabulary and lots of clever rhymes, and he might sing very fast and never repeat himself so that it's hard to tell he's lying.

How is songwriting related to writing? Did you ever want to be a writer?

I do also write fiction, and the biggest difference between writing fiction and writing songs is the length. In a short story, you have twenty to thirty pages to say what you want to say, and of course in a novel you have 300 pages or maybe even more. But a song barely fills even one page, so every word matters. When I'm writing a song, at the end of six hours maybe I've only written fifty words. That's okay. When I'm writing a story, I have to remember not to be so picky with every word. In these situations, I find it helpful to freewrite—to just write down whatever comes into my head without stopping. I think it's very useful (and fun) for all writers to experiment with different kinds of writing, such as poems, plays, songs, movie scripts, and comics. Try it!

What was your first lyricist/songwriter job?

The first musical I wrote was called *Epitaph*, and it was a comedy about a sick woman in a hospital trying to convince her two troublesome Chinese-American daughters to do a good job with her funeral. (I know that doesn't sound very funny, but it was. Really.) The next musical I wrote was called *Rainbow Valley*, based on the seventh book in the *Anne of Green Gables* series by L. M. Montgomery. It's set in Canada in 1906, and it's about the four motherless children of an absent-minded minister who form a club to teach themselves how to behave better—but the results don't turn out like they plan!

What are your goals for your literary future?

Do you remember the books and movies that you really, really loved when you were a kid? I want to write those. My other goal is to write stories that have Asian or Asian-American main characters. (I am Taiwanese-American.) Right now there are a few good books that have Asian main characters, but I think it would be great if there were even more. This is also important for musicals and plays and movies, because very few scripts ask for an Asian actor. So all these excellent Asian actors end up in the same room auditioning for the role of "Martial Arts Instructor" or "Scientist Number Three." Wouldn't it be great if they could audition for the main character?

What advice would you give to a young writer interested in becoming a lyricist/songwriter?

The most important thing is to make sure you have enough time in your life to write. Give writing a lot of respect. Write for fun with other people. Ask your friends to critique your work, but always ignore a few things they say; otherwise, it will be obvious that you were trying to please everybody and your work will be boring. Read lots of books on writing, like this one. Find books that tell you where to send your work when you're done with it, whether it's to magazines, theaters, contests, or publishers. Use the internet to make your work public, like on your own webpage or on YouTube or in online magazines. If you want to write songs, buy *The New Comprehensive American Rhyming Dictionary* by Sue Young and take it with you everywhere. It will serve you well. (For example, it just told me that "Sloppy Joe" rhymes with "Michelangelo.")

Do you think reading helps you with your job?

YES! Whenever I'm discouraged with my own writing and I can't think why anyone would *possibly* want to read anything I've written, I pick up a good book and it reminds me why writers are so important.

What are your favorite reads?

I read a lot of fantasy novels, such as Robin McKinley's *The Hero and the Crown*, Orson Scott Card's *Ender's Game*, Philip Pullman's *The Ruby in the Smoke*, Holly Black's *Tithe*, and Lev Grossman's *The Magicians*.

Name some of the authors who have inspired you and why.

Every writer is a conquering hero as far as I'm concerned, and there are many who inspire me. Ruth Ozeki wrote a book called *My Year of Meats* that I greatly admire for the following reason: It has an environmental message—but, even more importantly, it's *interesting*. I think writers have great power to spread a message to a wide audience, but you can't spread a message if your audience is bored. I think the best writers first concentrate on writing a great story that makes people laugh and hold their breath wondering what happens next—and only later do people realize that, hiding inside that great story, there is also a powerful message.

4

Choosing Your Topic: What Will You Write About?

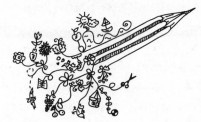

*Y*ou are sitting on a train when all of a sudden a story about a young wizard pops into your head. You jot down some notes and before you know it, you've plotted out seven whole books without writing even one word of the story. When you do finish the first book, you're so broke you can only afford to make two copies of it, so you send it to just two publishers. But luckily, one of the publishers loves it, and before you can say "Hogwarts," you are one of the most famous writers in the world!

Sound like a fantasy? Well, that is exactly how J. K. Rowling got started! For some writers, nothing is worse than staring at an empty piece of paper trying to decide what to write about. Choosing your topic doesn't always come as easily as it did to the creator of Harry Potter. In the beginning, the best thing to do is to write about what's on your mind. Even if it seems to be junk, just start writing. *Later,* when you've got the creative juices flowing, you can zero in on where you want to go with your ideas, how long you want your piece to be, why you're writing this particular story, and where you might want to publish it. The important thing to remember at the start is that *you don't have to have it all figured out to start writing.* Just start writing.

> Setting up a personal blog is a great tool in discovering topics that you care to write about. Use it as a place to test your creative writing. You don't have to have a theme on your blog, except maybe the theme of "what's on your mind." This way you can practice all sorts of writing styles while setting a commitment to completing each writing experience and posting them for readers and feedback. One day you might write an investigative report on what's really going on in the school kitchen and on another day you may try your hand at writing a whimsical short story of adventure featuring characters who resemble you and your best friends. In the end you will find that the posts you enjoy reading yourself are most likely the subjects you should concentrate on.

The Old Rule Still Stands: Write What You Know

You have probably already heard teachers or writers give the advice to "write what you know." That's difficult advice for many young writers, since they often think that they don't have enough life experience to write about anything! The fact is, you know a lot.

Just think about all the adult authors who write young adult and teen books—do you think they all *really* remember what it was like to be your age? Or know what it's like to be a kid now? How *can* they know? You actually know more about that topic than most adult authors do. What else do you know about?

Your journal can be a great place to find story ideas. If you've been keeping one, look over your entries and you'll start noticing words, phrases, and even patterns of topics that you can use as story starters, article topics, or poetry refrains. Check your journal or blog for these potential topic goldmines:

- What's been on your mind lately?

- Do you have a hobby or activity that you have lots of information on and like to talk about?

- Did something happen to make you really happy recently?

- Did something happen that made you very sad?

- Do you have a story from your life that friends always ask you to tell?

- Did you pass someone on the street today who prompted you to look twice and wonder what he or she was up to?

Think about what you know or observe about normal, everyday things and write about them from *your* point of view. When you write them down and share them with others, you will discover that what you know may be quite different from what other people know—and may be very interesting to them, as well.

When you first start writing, the most important thing is to get your ideas written down. Don't worry about things like spelling and grammar. Don't even be concerned about the order of your paragraphs. Later, you can revise and change the order of things, as well as proofread for spelling and grammar mistakes.

Whatever you do, *don't throw anything away*. It's better to make a folder for each topic you decide to write about and then date and save everything you write about it…even if you hate it. It may feel very dramatic and satisfying to crumple up a page and toss it in the trash, but that's not a very smart thing for a writer to do. Stephen King so hated his novel *Carrie*, the story of an unpopular girl who uses her telepathic powers to get revenge on teasing classmates, he threw it in the garbage! Luckily, his wife rescued the story and convinced Stephen to send it to publishers. *Carrie* became his first published novel and made Stephen King rich and famous. And it almost didn't make it past the garbage can! You can use *everything* you write, even if it's only to learn what you did wrong.

> *If you love singing, play an instrument, or if you just love music in general, you may find it fun to try your hand at writing lyrics. Pull song lyrics off the internet or from your CDs and take a look at what your favorite artists are singing about.*

Top Ten Things to Do When Searching for Inspiration:

1. DO consider yourself a writer. As long as you write, you are a writer.
2. DO write what you feel like writing, even if it seems terrible at the time. Try freewriting random words and ideas that pop into your head.
3. DO reread your journal, notes, scribbles, online status updates, and blog entries.
4. DO make lists of things you know about, even the ones that seem boring. (Who knows, they may be fascinating to other people!)
5. DO write real dialogue from your own life, but change it to suit the characters in your story.
6. DO include smells, sounds, and colors . . . even the not-so-pretty ones.
7. DO write down your dreams every morning. There could be some great stories there.
8. DO listen to the people around you. What's bugging them? What are they talking about? Write about that.
9. DO write down single sentences. Even if you don't have a story yet, you may think up a great sentence. Write it down and save it for later. The right story for it will come.
10. DO describe your characters. Like the single sentence, a character may form in your head before the story does. No

worries—just describe him or her in detail and save it for when the story comes later.

Top Ten Things Not to Do When Searching for Inspiration:

1. DON'T use erasers or Wite-Out; don't delete or scratch out.
2. DON'T focus on where it's going to end up, whether it will be published, or whether it's any good.
3. DON'T say, "This stinks."
4. DON'T crumple up pages or throw anything away.
5. DON'T watch TV, play video games, or go online while you're writing! If you need a break, take a walk.
6. DON'T distract yourself with the phone, texting, or email. Save these until you're finished with your writing time.
7. DON'T give in to distraction by suddenly deciding to clean your room.
8. DON'T worry about spelling, grammar, organization, or logic.
9. DON'T doubt yourself as a writer.
10. DON'T give up!

Focus on the writing and expressing what you feel inside and don't worry about the rest. Still stumped for a topic to write about? Never fear! Just try your hand at a few of the fun writing exercises in the next chapter.

Young Author Profile:
Zakiyyah Madyun

Pittsburgh, Pennsylvania, native **Zakiyyah Madyun** attended the School for the Creative and Performing Arts, which helped her explore her love of music, which she finds an inspiration. She writes both poetry and prose. She wrote the the following poem when she was fourteen years old.

No Such Thing as Silence
Poetry

My name speaks for me,
when I never asked to be spoken for.
It says it was made up.
It says I'm not from around here, am I?
It says my words will be laced with a thick accent.
It says I speak in foreign tongues,
and foreign tongues are confusing, aren't they?
It lies sometimes,
but what can I say to the assumptions it makes,
when I haven't said a thing?
Then my skin chimes in.
It says that I listen to rap music.
It says my words often come out slurred
and distorted.
It says I don't know much of nothing, do I?
Sometimes it lies.
The book that I'm holding asks for a few words.
It says I'll look down when I speak.
It says my voice will come out high and chiming.
It says I'm a mystery.
It says I want things to stay that way.
Music tells me I'm trying to be something that I'm not.
It tells me to sit down,
and listen to something more appropriate for
people like me, you know.
It asks me why I don't like what they like.
It says I could, couldn't I?
It says I'd like it if I tried.
I don't answer.
My arms and legs revolt against me,

saying that I ought to have some rhythm.

They scold me,

as though talents can be condensed,

and referred to as simply genetic.

I try to make them understand,

but my limbs say otherwise,

taking honesty for modesty.

But the worst liar of all is voice,

warping my words,

making serious sentiments sound lighter.

Morphed by age into something that isn't,

quite,

right.

Rumors are spread,

and the truth lies damaged

in a desolate corner,

because it can't decide whether or not it has anything to

prove.

It's used to abandonment.

They see my face,

my skin,

hear my name,

listen to the tone of my voice,

but no one ever sees,

ever hears, or smells or tastes

the truth

that's right in front of their faces,

and it's a shame,

honesty.

So clear, so clean,

you see right through it,

without a backwards glance.

5

Writing Exercises: How to Get Unstuck Fast

You're curled up in your favorite writing chair with your computer nestled comfortably in your lap. Yes! You are ready to write. You are dying to enter that contest or submit a story to that magazine—whatever. Write your brains out! You're sure that the words will start rushing out any minute and that you will be ready to catch them. Here they come . . . any minute now . . . you're still waiting. Aargh! Nothing's happening!

Writer's Block

You've probably already heard the dreaded term *writer's block*. It happens when writers just can't get their writing to go right or even put pencil to paper. One writer described it as "staring at a blank piece of paper that stares right back at me in silence." Some writers, like Dean Koontz, Todd Strasser, Laurie Halse Anderson, and Phyllis Reynolds Naylor, are very methodical and produce a new book (or more) every year or two. Other authors take much longer. But every author experiences writer's block—the feeling that your mind is as dry as the Mojave Desert! If you get stuck, don't worry. You're in good company. Just like any writer, you will have to figure out a way to get past it. A great way to leap past your writer's block is to try some fun writing exercises. Try one of these and you will feel better fast and have pages of lovely words to show for it.

Ten Writing Prompts

Have you ever heard of a *stage prompt*? During a play, there is always one person with a copy of the script who sits in front of the stage and whispers lines to actors who forget what they're supposed to say next. This is called prompting. All an actor usually needs is the first few words of his speech, and then he's off and running. A writing prompt works the same way. It gives you the start of an idea to take off from in your own writing. Here are some writing prompts that will easily help you get unstuck fast:

1. Behind-the-Scenes Fairy Tale

Write a fairy tale, from a character's point of view, that explains his or her personal issues (which you will invent). For example, you could become the wolf in "Three Little Pigs" who just wants the pigs to stop building on his front lawn. Or the mouse in "Cinderella" who feels ridiculous to be all dressed up in human clothes and driving a pumpkin. Or Grumpy the Dwarf whose chronic depression is made worse when that dumb girl invades his house.

2. Man, I Loved That...

Warm up your creative muscles by writing a review of the last movie, concert, or sports game that you saw. Write about not only your opinion, but about how the audience around you reacted.

3. Reality Field Trip

Take yourself on a field trip and interview someone in your town: a firefighter, gas station owner, school custodian, EMT, or mail carrier. Jot down a few simple questions ahead of time, like, "What gave you the idea to do this job?" "Was it tough at first?" "What do you like about it?" "Have you learned anything about our town as a result of your job?" "What advice would you have for young people who might want to go into your field?" Then just listen and take as many notes as you can.

Young Author Profile:
Jemma Leech

Jemma Leech is a British Texan. At age thirteen, while at school in Houston, she pursued her passions of writing, reading, and going on adventures. She wrote this article on Gary Paulsen in 2009.

"Read Like a Wolf Eats," Gary Paulsen Tells Young Readers

Journalism

Gary Paulsen balances his cap on his head. Pulling the peak down over his clear blue eyes, he appears to be shielding them from the glare of public attention as much as from the bright lights of the Pershing auditorium. This man is the author of 200 books and the winner three times of the Newbery Honor, yet he looks more like a cross between Daniel Boone, Captain Ahab, and Santa.

Best known for tales of wilderness survival and husky dogsled races, he writes from his own experiences. As a young boy in Minnesota, with a difficult home life, he took to the woods to trap game and to fish, just to get food to live. These skills form the basis of the *Hatchet* series in which a boy has to learn to survive in the wilderness after a plane crash.

Paulsen said, "I have done everything I wrote about in *Hatchet*—trapping, fishing, hunting, even two forced landings in planes. In the woods I was cool, I was the man."

He even offers tips to potential survivalists. "Beaver is the best meat of all—it tastes like beef but with 37 percent protein. Beef only has about 25 percent."

He completed two Iditarods, the grueling 1,100-mile dogsled race across Alaska, and was devoted to one of his lead dogs, Cookie, in particular.

"Cookie was the best thing that ever happened to me; she saved my life several times. I have a picture of Cookie in my wallet, but not one of my wife. Go figure!"

Smiling at the memory, he recalls that it was during his time training and racing the dogs that he wrote his three Newbery Honor books, *Dogsong* (1985), *Hatchet* (1987), and *The Winter Room* (1989). So does he write from the back of the dogsled? Almost.

"I write all the time, wherever I am—on an airplane, in the kennels, on the boat, at my ranch. I carry my laptop with me all the time and when that's not practical, I write longhand on pads of paper. I'm a writer who runs dogs; I'm a writer who sails. I'm a writer—it's what I do, it's who I am."

Jack-of-all-trades in life and in writing, Paulsen writes books ranging from adventure stories like *Hatchet* to historical settings like his newest book, *Woods Runner*, set during America's war of independence. He also writes humor, with the follow-up to *Lawn Boy*, his tale of economic success in a twelve-year-old's lawn-mowing business, published this spring. So which does he prefer, humor or drama?

"Writing is about work and about love, whether it's humor or drama, and I don't find one easier than the other. Alternating them makes for a nice change of pace, but I never decide to write a funny or a serious book. I just start writing and it becomes what it is."

Paulsen is keen to pass on his own wild brand of advice to young writers too. "Read like a wolf eats. Read everything you can get your hands on and write every single day. The discipline of reading and writing every day will be valuable."

So whether he is running his snow dogs, sailing the high seas, or surviving in the wild woods, Gary Paulsen is first and foremost a writer. "I write because I love to write. I would write even if I didn't get published. I will die writing."

His legion of readers hopes that won't be for a very long time. Gary Paulsen gave his readers' talk in the Pershing auditorium as part of the literary organization Inprint's *Cool Brains!* series. For more information, visit inprinthouston.org/cool-brains-series.

4. A "Secret" Conversation

Make a list of at least ten secrets, wishes, and/or problems that your friends have. Next, create two fictional characters and give each of them one of these secrets, wishes, or problems. Finally, write a dialogue between your two characters. Write it like a script, using initials for the character's names and starting a new line each time there's a new speaker. Don't write any description or background; just write what they say to each other. Make their words express their secrets, wishes, or problems.

> You can't be a writer if you're not writing, so just write. Whether freestyle or structured, as with a writing exercise, as long as you're writing something, you're moving in the right direction. Practice makes perfect (or at least better!).

5. Acrostic Poetry

Although *acrostic* might sound like a disease, it's actually guaranteed to fill up a page with writing! An acrostic poem starts with a word, phrase, or name—it could be your name, a character in a book, or even your favorite cookie.

Write the word down the left side of your page, one letter at a time on each line. This is your poem's *spine word*. Then use the letter on each line as the first letter of the first word on that line, and keep writing after that word to complete the line. Don't worry about making your poem rhyme. It just needs to relate to your spine word. Lines can run from one line to the next, so each line doesn't have to be a complete sentence. Here are a few samples. Look for the spine words:

> **A**nimals are irresistible
> **N**othing beats their furry little faces
> **I**mpossible not to love
> **M**ust be animals!
> **A**dorable, everyone wants one …
> **L**ost in their own dream world all day long.
>
> —*Antonia Sohns, age 12*

> **P**owerful words written together,
> **O**ften staying in a person's heart forever
> **E**ven if they are not wanted. Poems are like
> **M**usic to the heart and food for the
> **S**oul.
>
> —*Zoe Novendster, age 13*

6. Fabulous Fables

A fable is a story that usually has animal characters and a lesson at the end. Remember the story about the tortoise and the hare? That's a fable. The hare is fast, but overconfident that he will win the race. The tortoise is slow, but persistent and humble. When the tortoise wins the race, the moral is "Slow and steady wins the race."

You can write your own fable using animals with human characteristics. Start with a wise saying (such as "Look before you leap," "A fool and his money are soon parted," and so on) and build your story from there. Consider which animals would best represent the human virtues and vices you've chosen: a fox could be sly, an owl wise, a sheep dumb, a butterfly concerned with beauty, and so on.

Another way to create your own fable is to write a story about something that happened to you in real life, but replace the people with animals that have the best and worst characteristics of the real people involved. By turning a true story into an animal fable, you can say almost anything you want. Just be sure to change the names, or your sister Anna may not be too happy when she reads your fable "Anna the Annoying Aardvark"!

7. Can't Touch, Taste, Smell, Hear, or See It, But...

An *abstract* concept is something you can't use your senses to perceive; you can't touch it, taste it, smell it, hear it, or see it. Anger, love, greed, envy, happiness, value, selfishness, thoughtfulness, and rudeness are just a few abstract concepts. Pick an abstract concept and make it come alive—make it a character with a name and an appearance. This character should totally represent the abstract concept through his other appearances, actions, and speeches. Then have your abstract character join a baseball team, lunch table, or trip to the mall. Tell the story from there. How does this person affect everyone around him? What kinds of trouble might he get into?

A variation on this idea is to bring a season to life. What if Summer, the new girl in school, strolled into your homeroom one wintry morning. What would happen? Or how about a land where each season lives? The season's personality and appearance could match its season—Summer might be warm and loving, while Winter is icy and distant. Just think of the interesting conflicts that could arise!

8. Memoirs-R-Us

A memoir is a story based on a memory. Think of a story from your own childhood, especially a really funny, sad, or scary one. When you write it down, tell it as clearly as you can, even if you can't remember every detail. Write in the first person ("I remember...")

or the third person ("Cathy woke up that morning...). Write as much as you can, as fast as you can. Next, go back and add a few conversations and details, like colors, smells, and sounds. You will be amazed at how official your little story sounds now—the one you've known so well that it never seemed worth writing down. Until now...

9. Odes to the Ordinary

An ode is a long, formal poem that is meant to be a serious song of praise. Odes usually praise a person, thing, or idea that is highly distinguished or admirable. Odes also have a reputation for being serious, intellectual, and ... well ... stuffy. That's why writing an un-stuffy ode about something completely ordinary can be lots of fun. Award-winning poet Pablo Neruda once wrote a wonderful poem called "Ode to My Socks." In it, he describes his socks in great detail, as well as his thoughts about the person who knitted them.

You can choose something or someone that you know very well, and write a poem or prose poem (a poem in paragraph form that doesn't rhyme) that goes into great detail about it. You don't have to gush; just point out the traits you think deserve praise. Although it isn't necessary to rhyme, you should try to use some formal words ("thou dost" = "you do," "thou art" = "you are," "enwrapped" = "wrapped up," and so on) to contrast with the not-so-formal subject of your poem. Here are some ode ideas to get you started:

Ode to ...

- *My Running Shoes*

- *My Math Teacher*

- *My Teddy Bear*

- *My Skateboard*

- *Final Exams*

- *My Karate Belt*

- *My Cat*

- *Little Brothers*

- *Flannel Pajamas*

- *The Cartoon Network*

When in doubt, clear it out. A healthy "brain dump" is highly effective for wrangling your worries as well as your ideas. Take that blank piece of paper in front of you and make a list of what's blocking you. Is it fear, stress about home-work, a fight with a friend? Seeing your concerns in print can reestablish your perspective while creating a handy "To be continued . . ." list for later. Once you feel cleared, the words may come. If they don't, however, don't fret! Do the same brain dump for your ideas, writing down everything that comes to mind. Many times you'll find that you're actually less stuck than you realized, and your muse will return.

10. You've Got Mail!

Well, you will get mail if you send some first! Write a letter to your favorite author or politician about an issue that's important to you. It's pretty exciting to get a letter back from the president of the United States, a member of the U.S. Senate, Jodi Picoult, or Nathaniel Philbrick—and we know lots of kids who have!

Be sure to include your name and address in the top right-hand corner of the page, plus your full name and signature at the bottom of the letter. Visit personal websites to see if they have a P.O. box to send mail to or even a Q&A email address to send your thoughts to. Or you can send author letters to their publishers.

You'll find the publisher's address inside the author's book, on the copyright page (usually on the back side of the title page). To find addresses for government officials, check online.

In your letter, don't be afraid to state your true opinion, even if you didn't like part of an author's book or you disagree with a politician's beliefs on a certain issue. But remember to always be respectful or the reader won't finish reading your letter and your efforts will be wasted.

In a letter to an author, you might write:

- about your favorite books by that author

- why you like those particular books best

- questions about the author's characters or plots

- questions about how the author got certain ideas

- why you like to write—and ask for advice!

- a thank you for writing such books and for reading your letter

In a letter to a politician, you might write:

- about an issue that concerns you

- why you are concerned about it

- how you got interested in the issue

- what you think the politician should do about it

- questions about what the politician has already done on that issue

- a thank you for considering your ideas

Ten Writing Props

Each of these exercises requires a prop that can be found anywhere: a photo, a pet rock, or a good people-watching spot. This time, the prop is the key that will unlock your creativity. Follow these directions and you'll be writing fabulous stories before you know it!

1. Writing from a Photo

A photograph is a story frozen in time, just waiting for someone to release it. You can be that someone! Look through your own photo albums, magazines, or postcards. Choose a photo and climb into it, walk around in it, and imagine as many details as you can. If there are people in your photo, *become* one of them. What are you thinking? What just happened?

Write from different points of view: the third person ("It was so hot the maple leaves drooped. Maggie sat under her tree and untied her sneakers ... "), the first person ("It was so hot that day the leaves on my thinking tree drooped straight down. I sat in its shade and took off my sneakers to cool down."), or both ... some surprising things might surface!

2. Use an Author as a Model

Copying the style of your favorite author isn't always cheating. It can even be a great help for getting started with your writing. Try looking at the first few paragraphs of a favorite book. Choose three sentences and copy them, substituting new names and mostly new verbs, nouns, adjectives, and adverbs. Keep the basic sentence structure the same. Here's an example from *Alice's Adventures in Wonderland*:

> Alice was beginning to get very tired of sitting by her sister on the bank, and of having nothing to do ... when suddenly a white rabbit with pink eyes ran close by her. There was nothing so *very* remarkable in that; nor did Alice think it so very much out of the way to hear the Rabbit say to itself, "Oh, dear! Oh, dear! I shall be late!" But when the Rabbit actually

took a watch out of his waistcoat pocket, and looked at it, and then hurried on, Alice started to her feet ...

And here's a new version, with names, verbs, and so on changed (the new words are in *italics*):

Jason was beginning to get very *bored* of sitting by *his step-father* on the *bench,* and of *throwing stale bread to some dirty old pigeons* . . . when suddenly a *black squirrel* with *blue* eyes ran *across his sneaker.* There was nothing *sooooo weird about* that; nor did *Jason* think it *sooooo strange* to hear the *squirrel* say to itself *in an angry voice, "Oh yeah, sure, that's just what we need!!"* But when the *squirrel* actually *pulled a cell phone out of its fanny pack, flipped it open, started to mumble into it, and scampered on, Jason jumped* to *his* feet.

In the first version, Lewis Carroll draws us into his fascinating story in just a few lines. The new story has some similarities, but it's clear we're in new territory—a new character and plot are being hatched. Keep going after you've written these first few sentences, using your author as a model whenever you'd like.

A Note on Plagiarism

It's fine to create your own unique version of someone else's essay, poem, or story (like the popular mash-ups *Pride & Prejudice & Zombies* and *Alice in Zombieland*), so long as you make sure to acknowledge your source. After the title or at the end of your new piece, write whom you got your inspiration from: "Modeled on Lewis Carroll's *Alice's Adventures in Wonderland*" or "From headlines in the *Vineyard Gazette,* July 23, 2011."

This technique is like learning to ride a bike: At first, you need someone to hold the back of your seat. But once you get going, you can do it all by yourself. Once you've gotten started, let go of the original author's plot and characters, and let your story go off on its own adventure.

3. Found Poems

Want to write a poem but can't think of any good words or phrases? Try stealing some! This is actually legal—and expected!—when you write *found poetry*. (Of course, you have to acknowledge your source with a *citation* at the end of the poem.) This technique is a lot like those magnetic poetry kits, but you use paper and scissors (or the cut-and-paste function on your computer).

The idea behind writing found poems is to find language that is NOT trying to be poetic and reshape it into your own poem. Look for writing in textbooks, appliance directions, or boring newspaper articles. Once you've chosen a piece of writing to work with, copy down thirty to eighty words and/or phrases by hand or on your computer. Next, cut out the words and phrases and start rearranging them in front of you, keeping words you like and discarding those you don't like. Eventually you'll see your words shaping themselves into new meanings and ideas.

Your poem doesn't have to rhyme or have a specific rhythm. Feel free to change verb tenses, change endings to singular or plural, and change pronouns to fit he/she or they/them/it kinds of problems. You can repeat lines, words, or phrases as you see fit, and you can insert or change punctuation to help your reader understand your meaning.

Although strict found poems require that you not add *any* words, this is *your* poem, after all, so allow yourself two new words. But only two. Give your found poem a title and put your name at the bottom of the poem and *be sure to write where you found the words.* Here are a few found poems written by kids:

Learning a Language

The future of Latin in the United States
Relies on this book.

Enlightened upper grades in our elementary school have

Even those who recognize the wisdom
Of justification

Our own experience in school
Was bad

So we want to make it
As bad for you

Here in the most difficult
To understand Latin Book
Ever written

Have FUN
And remember
Modern Languages don't mean anything
LATIN IS LIFE.

—*Sam Sack, age 13*

(From the preface to *Preparatory Latin Book I, 2nd edition* by
William J. Buehner & John Ambrose. NY: Longman, 1977.)

The Wonderful World of Plastic

We see plastic objects every day

Dishes and bowls
A toy and garden hose.

Drying or cooling
It will retain shape.

Plastic—natural
Clay, glass, and rubber

From pine trees and nitric acid
More practical than a surgeon

Returning to England in 1843
With some kind of knife.

Plastic in a toothbrush company
And in buttons and combs.

Plastics, the man-made miracle.

—*Mary Charlotte Borgen, age 13*

(Words were taken from *Plastics: The Man-Made Miracle* by Walter
Buehr. NY: William Morrow & Co., 1967.)

4. Journal Jewels

Use your journal. Okay, this tidbit of advice comes as no surprise,
but this time, try using it in a new way. Read through it with a
highlighter in hand, highlighting words and phrases that are especially strong, surprising, or beautiful. If you're using a computer,
you can electronically highlight the phrases with color or copy
and paste them into a new document. Make a list of these "jewels"
and use a few in a poem, as the key words in the first sentence of a
story, or as part of a dialogue for a character in a story.

5. Pet Rock

Rocks are like snowflakes—no two are alike. And for you, no
two have the same story. Go outside and find a rock about the size
of your fist. Look at it carefully and turn it over in your hands.
Think about what might be inside if you were able to crack it
open. Imagine you could shrink and walk on and into your rock—
what would you see? Write down the details of your rock world.
Describe the environment, any creatures that live there, how they
survive, how they communicate. Keep going—this kind of thing
can get pretty magical ... for just a rock!

6. Halloween All Year

When you write about a character, you are actually putting on a
mask and creating his or her voice and movements and feelings.

Sometimes a real mask can get you going in directions you never considered. Look around your house, ask friends, or visit a party or costume shop and find a few interesting masks.

Put your mask on, look at yourself in the mirror, and start talking in your new *persona* (role). Write down what your character might say if talking to others. Then write what she might say to herself—the truth about how she feels about herself and what she must do in her life. Use this character and your observations as the basis of a story.

7. Spin Off a Missing Chapter

Take a favorite book and write a chapter that the author left out. You might focus on a minor character, giving readers his point of view, or you might reveal behind-the-scenes details that you create. You could come up with a surprising new short story. In television, this is called a *spin-off*.

A variation on this idea is to write a new prologue (events that happened before the story begins) or epilogue (a summary of everything that happens to each character after the book ends) for the famous story.

Lots of people enjoy this sort of writing, often called *fan fiction*. There are many websites where teens and adults share their fan-fiction stories and give each other feedback. If you find a group of people online sharing fan-fiction stories about your favorite book and would like to join in, just remember to be safe! Many fan-fiction authors use pseudonyms (false names) so that they don't have to give out their real names online.

8. Smell-O-Rama

The sense of smell has been proven to be the quickest path to memory. So why not take a field trip down memory lane, via the spice cabinet in your kitchen? Sit down with a pen and paper and a few spice jars, and smell the contents. Choose one and get lost in the memories or images that come to you. Write about what the smell reminds you of and soon a poem or a memoir will start magically forming as the scents waft around you.

9. Memories in the Attic

Go into your attic or hallway closet and dig out a few of your old toys. Play with some of them—bounce the pink ball, open up the game Operation, pull the string of the Buzz Lightyear doll. Free-write about how you felt about the toy. Were there special rules you made up? Was it your favorite for a while? Did you get it at a birthday party? Which one?

Or *become* the toy and write in the first person using the toy's voice. Tell the reader what it's like to be the poor guy in the game Operation or the over-pulled Buzz Lightyear doll.

Maintain a regular writing routine. As you know, distractions are everywhere—especially when you're stuck with writer's block. Having an established habit (time, location, and so on) combats mental noise and procrastination to unleash your creative flow. So, keep a reliable, cleared space in your schedule to maximize your genius and effectiveness.

10. Write a Script Based on Someone Else's Story

Hollywood does this all the time! Take your favorite story and turn it into a play or movie. At the start of each scene, write in italics how the stage is set and what props are to be used. (Remember, the audience won't hear these words, but the director will use them to set the stage and guide the actors.)

Write the name of each character, in capital letters, before his or her lines. In regular print, write the lines to be spoken out loud. Directions to actors should be enclosed in parentheses before or after their lines.

Follow the story closely and feel free to use words from the story's dialogue. You will have to change most of the descriptions into actions or dialogue spoken by the actors. Some of the story can be changed into stage directions, which you will write in italics. This way, the reader can tell the difference between words that the actors say out loud and the actions that they do or the sights the audience sees.

This is a great exercise to do and then act out with friends. But don't forget to always acknowledge your source—the title, author, publisher, and year of publication.

When You're Not Totally Broken Down, Just a Bit Stalled...

There will be times when you won't need to launch into a whole writing exercise. Perhaps you have a great idea already, but at the moment, your mind seems to be a blank wall. Those words you just had in your mind seem to have flown out the window. Try these mini–writer's block cures.

Walk Away

When you feel you have nothing left to write, take a break. Go shoot some hoops or take a long walk with the dog. When you're not thinking about your writing, you may find that the next paragraph suddenly appears in your head. One writer busts her writer's block in the car. She puts on her favorite music and just relaxes. Sooner or later she gets unstuck, pulls over, and jots down her thoughts.

Start in the Middle...Or at the End

Sometimes you may have a great idea but not a great first sentence. Don't worry. There's no rule that says you have to start at the beginning. You could write your ending first or start somewhere in the middle. You could start your story by writing a really interesting scene or character instead of the beginning. Whatever works for you is just fine.

Keep Souvenirs

If you are writing a story, it can help to keep something on your desk or in your pocket that inspires you—a photograph or some object that reminds you of one of your characters.

Use scissors.
(Just don't run with them!)

What if you like what you've written, but it doesn't seem to be in the right order? Well, there's always that wonderful computer tool called "cut and paste." But sometimes it helps to physically move your paragraphs around too. Try this: print out your writing with enough space between paragraphs that you can actually cut them up. After cutting them apart, take your pieces and spread them out on the floor or a large table. Then move your text around and hear how it sounds. After you've rearranged it, you can go back to the computer and copy the rearrangements.

And Don't Forget to Recycle:
Save Everything!

Did you write anything with the prompts or props in this chapter? If you did, good for you! You probably have some great stories or poems already started. No matter what you think of them, save all of your first attempts. When you reread your writing later, chances are you'll be saying something like, *Hey, did I write this? Not too shabby!* Your writing will seem fresh and unique—and maybe even good enough to send to publishers. And we'll tell you how to do just that in the coming chapters!

Young Author Profile:
Jesse Shulman

Seventeen-year-old **Jesse Shulman** is from Toronto, Ontario. As an aspiring filmmaker and novelist, he is interested in framing small details of life in ways that make them resonate with an audience.

Split Ends
Personal Essay/Memoir

Yesterday I saw her in the street. Her hair looked slept in, split ends and all.

In another age, when I was eight and she was nine, we wanted to be astrophysicists or inventors. We built a robo-body for Stephen Hawking out of Legos, and a voicebox too, by downloading sound clips from Bogart movies and putting them on a tape recorder, so Hawking could sound like Humphrey. We planned to create guitars that played themselves, so nerds could flip a switch and be cool. We designed connector cords for brains out of USB ports and copper wire, so everyone could open their minds and let others in, so parents wouldn't fight over miscommunications, so old people wouldn't be lonely, too embarrassed to call their children.

Two years passed. Like most girls, she developed fast. I didn't. She raised her anchor, sails unfurled, and I lost her to the horizon; I guess she wanted a new world and figured it was where I wasn't.

"You're such a boy." She smiled while she said it, which confused me.

You know when you play the same scene over until you're not sure if you've changed the script? I asked why she wanted to go. She said she didn't know, that she just wanted to be normal, just regular and boring like everyone else.

"But nobody's boring," I said. She smiled again, which confused me.

Maybe it was when I told her we'd govern an underwater city in a glass dome, where no one starved because of octopi farms and no one was sad, because all the architecture was crisp and colorful, built off blueprints by Haussmann, Hundertwasser, and Gehry. All policies would be egalitarian, and there'd be no glass ceilings (except literally, of course).

Maybe it was when I told her we'd reboot the hot air balloon as the mode of public transport, so everyone could see the world from up high without looking down on one another; we'd be the first reporters to secure an exclusive tell-all with God; we'd start a family in Antarctica and breed mammoths back into existence to be our pets.

Antarctica is cold, she said.

So we drifted, like jetsam. We split.

When I was seventeen, she was eighteen and heading off for university in Paris. We'd only been talking a few times a month, if that. Sometimes we'd go out: I'd text her to bring running shoes, an attitude for adventure, and always—always—a towel. We'd meet downtown. I'd give us both fake names and fedoras, and we'd pretend to be detectives, asking people on the sidewalk for clues. We'd see tourist sites in our own city and perform short, silent plays in front of security cameras. Sometimes she'd bring me to her parties, where, ironically, she'd be the one feeling out of place. She'd get jealous if girls crowded me, especially if they were laughing, especially if they had low-cut tops and no split ends.

To me, her imperfections were what made her perfect. I'm not sure if she ever got that.

Usually she'd just come over. We'd cuddle and talk in bed about how the universe was expanding, how stars that burnt out years ago still felt real, how our DNA allowed for forty billion possible people who could've been born in our place, and we owed it to them to make our lives mean something. We'd turn on a movie we'd never seen, press mute, and improvise dialogue.

During her university send-off, we were standing by an intersection and the light went green. She kissed my cheek and whispered something over her shoulder as I walked away; it got lost in honks of traffic. She covered her eyes, turned a corner, and was gone.

Sometimes shoes feel waterlogged, even though they're not.

I felt lost in space. And time. And plain old lost.

Sometimes, reading Stephen Hawking or Richard Dawkins, life becomes microscopic.

I felt like a rocket man because astronauts' tears hang in zero gravity and stay there, like memories, floating, drifting. In space, if you want to get rid of tears before they seep into the wiring and the ship sparks apart, you stick them in Tupperware. You hide them until one day there are too many and the box bursts.

The universe is expanding.

Yesterday I saw her in the street. She was in town for the weekend. Her hair looked slept in, split ends and all. We had coffee on a park bench and watched people pass by like in a Woody Allen movie.

A couple on a tandem bike rolled past on the grass. I looked at her.

"You can't breed mammoths back to life," she said.

"You can try."

I looked at her and gave my Humphrey Bogart impression:

"I was born when she kissed me. I died when she left me. I lived a few weeks while she loved me."

She cast her eyes down to the coffee between her thighs. The steam rose and warmed her cheeks. Or maybe she was blushing.

She looked up and smiled.

I looked at her.

She looked at me.

"We can try."

The Process: Writing and Rewriting

kay, you're glued to your keyboard and the words are coming out fast and furious! You've decided your genre. You even have a great topic in mind. In fact, you have a great character, a great beginning, and a knock-'em-dead ending. This book should be finished by dinnertime, no problem! Well, just as soon as you figure out what goes between the beginning and the end, that is!

How long does it take to write a masterpiece? A day? A weekend? Ten years? Yes, yes, and yes. There's no telling how long it will take to write a really great book. Author Margaret Wise Brown wrote *Goodnight Moon* in a weekend, and it became one of the bestselling children's books ever written. On the other hand, some writers spend their whole lives writing *just one book*.

There's no right way to write a book, and there's no time limit either. Every writer discovers a process that works best for him or her, and each writer's process is unique. Yours will be too. But as you begin writing your masterpiece, keep in mind:

1. You will rewrite it later. No matter how fast they wrote it or how great it is, all writers polish their work.
2. You may get stuck. Every writer hits writer's block some-times. But don't worry…the tricks in chapter 5 will help you get unstuck.
3. It's okay to start all over again. Sometimes an idea just doesn't pan out, and it's better to move on to something new and fresh. That doesn't mean you won't come back to your old idea again, though, so don't throw it out! Stick it in one of your files to look at later. You never know—there may be something there after all.

The Writing Process

When inspiration strikes, you should begin writing immediately. Getting your initial thoughts recorded while the creative juices are flowing is critical. Otherwise, you may forget that amazing flash of brilliance. In fact, you probably will . . . that's why it's called a flash. Don't worry about anything besides putting your thoughts on paper: let the writing flow no matter if your words are mis-spelled or your punctuation is wrong. You can go back and fix these details later. Finally, always carry a notebook or a cell phone (most models have several options for capturing notes) in case the inspiration comes when you are not free to write.

What's a First Draft?

The term *first draft* sounds pretty serious, but it's not. It's just your first attempt at writing a story. Your first draft may be the framework of a story that you will fill in later. Or it could be a complete work that you won't change much during your rewrit-ing process. Your first draft can be handwritten on a pad of paper, typed on a computer, or even spoken into a voice recorder—whatever works best for you to get your thoughts out. Go for it. One writer wrote the first chapter of her book on a bunch of napkins on an airplane!

How Many Drafts Will I Do?

That's up to you, and again there is no right answer. Your first draft is for getting your thoughts down. Later drafts are for polishing your story—adding details, reworking scenes, making dialogue more realistic, and so on. Once you've written your first draft, put it away for a while—a day, a week . . . however long it takes until you can read it as if it were the first time you were reading it. You want to be able to come back and read it with fresh eyes. This will help you see where your writing needs work. Many writers also find it helpful to have a friend, teacher, or writer's group read their first drafts and give them comments on what is good and what could be improved (more on this in the next chapter).

Most writers will do at least two drafts before they feel their writing is finished. When you go back and reread your first draft, you may find a scene that just doesn't work or a character that doesn't quite fit in. Don't be afraid to cut material that doesn't work. It will make your writing stronger. But don't throw it away—that cut material may be the beginning of another story!

In writing this chapter of our book, for example, we started by writing the first draft in pencil on a big yellow legal pad. Next, we read it over and made notes and changes in the margin before typing it up. Then we put the first draft away for a week. When we came back to it, we made more improvements and fixed the grammar and spelling mistakes (we love spell-check!). After two or three drafts, we finally had a final draft of chapter 6 ready to send to our publisher.

Good Writing Structure: The Basics

We certainly don't want to tell you exactly how to write—that's the fun, creative part. But if you notice that your story doesn't really grab the reader and you want to add some zip to it, take a look at these basics of story structure:

Conflict

If you're writing a story, script, opinion piece, or essay, chances are that your writing needs a conflict—or a problem—to keep your reader's interest. A conflict is a struggle between two opposing forces. In a story, the conflict is usually between the main character (also called the *protagonist*) versus something external or internal:

External conflict: the main character is in conflict with something concrete, like another character (the Wicked Witch of the West, Darth Vader, annoying little sister, bully, and so on) or a force of nature (a tornado, the perfect storm, quicksand, and so on).

Internal conflict: the main character is struggling against something abstract, like a parent's expectations, peer pressure, society's morals, or even his own conscience. An internal conflict is a struggle within a character's heart or mind. Here are some good examples of internal conflicts your character might have:

- Whether or not to steal the leather jacket that he or she can't afford to buy but really, really wants.

- Being the first boy to join the school dance team or the first girl to join the football team.

- Going out with someone his or her parents hate.

Characters

Your story should have a *protagonist* (the main character) and an *antagonist* (the person, thing, or idea that causes the central conflict). You might also have minor characters who come in and out of your story as it progresses and who might even supply some minor conflicts. It helps to write down your characters' traits. Draw sketches of them to keep all their characteristics in mind as you write. As your story progresses and goes through revisions, remember to update those sketches too.

Here's a great form for remembering the important traits of your characters. Fill out a character sketch for each character in your story.

Character Sketch (Fill in the blanks)

name _____
(*Check out websites and library books for naming babies; they have cool names and their meanings.*)

gender _____

height _____

age _____

hair color _____

eye color _____

race _____

religion _____

fashion style_____

loves to _____

hates to _____

hopes to _____

favorite saying or word _____

pet peeve_____

Once you have sketched out the character of each person in your story, you can use these descriptions as details in your writing. Each trait can become a source of conflict in your story as well. You don't have to describe your characters directly to the reader to get their traits across. In fact, it's usually more interesting if your readers learn about a character in more subtle, indirect ways—by how other characters react to her, what they say about her, or by what the character says and does. Developing your characters is called *characterization*. Here's an example of how you might describe a character directly or indirectly:

Description: *Dorothy was a thoughtful girl who yearned for a more interesting life filled with adventure, friendship, and love.*

How others react: *The Cowardly Lion, the Tin Woodsman, and the Scarecrow left everything and followed Dorothy, knowing she might lead them to what they wanted and needed.*

What others say: *"Don't worry," said the Tin Woodsman to the Cowardly Lion, "Dorothy won't hurt you."*

What the character says or does: *"Why, you poor thing," Dorothy said. "You are all rusty. I'll help you. Where's the oil can?"*

Setting

The setting is the time and place in which your story is set. Go back and add as many details about your setting as you can. You might think your reader sees the same things you see in your head, but add the details anyway. Stimulate the senses: put in smells, tastes, sounds, feelings, and sights. Be sure that your reader has a clear sense of your story's setting from the beginning, or she will feel lost while reading it.

One young writer went back and added a fall setting to her story late in her writing process. By describing the red and yellow colors of the season, she was able to emphasize the fiery dangers lurking in her story's central conflict. Writers often use their setting as a metaphor or symbol for their conflict or their characters' feelings. For example, you may wish to have a storm brewing outside your main character's window to symbolize her struggle over what to do next and her feeling that trouble is coming.

Setting can be a great source of drama. Have you ever felt mysterious while walking through a fog? Or peaceful while basking in the sunshine? Your setting descriptions can be effective parallels to your character's feelings.

As with your characters, creating a setting sketch can help you better describe your setting.

Setting Sketch (Fill in the blanks)

year _____

time of day _____

location _____

sights/scenes _____

weather _____

smells _____

noises/sounds _____

physical feelings _____
   (scratchy sand beneath toes, biting wind against cheeks, stifling heat in the waiting room, and so on)

Plot

Unless you want your reader to be left unsatisfied, you should make sure that your story has a beginning, a middle, and an end.

And those three elements should be *balanced*. Too often, a writer starts out with lots of details and description at the beginning of his story, but by the end, he seems tired of writing, and the whole story gets solved too quickly to be interesting or believable.

The Beginning

Often called the *exposition*, the beginning is the part that gets the reader familiar with the basic characters, setting, and conflicts. You want to include an event that shows the reader what the conflict is (also called the *inciting incident*). Can you figure out the inciting incident in *The Wizard of Oz?*

> *Dorothy is bored on her farm in Kansas, has an unpleasant encounter with the witch-like librarian, and then a tornado whisks her and her house to the Land of Oz.*

The Middle

The middle is usually the longest part of the story and has three parts to it:

The build-up: This is the part of your story where you create tension (also called the *rising action*) and hook your readers into reading more. After the inciting incident, include some events that develop the conflict.

> *Dorothy lands in Oz, sets off on her journey, meets and befriends the Scarecrow, Tin Woodsman, and Cowardly Lion, battles the Wicked Witch, and so on.*

The climax or turning point: At this point, something *big* happens that brings the central conflict out into the open and gets other characters involved in it. Your reader should really know what the problem is and wonder how it will be solved.

> *Dorothy and her friends discover that the Wizard is a fake and may not be able to grant their wishes after all.*

Falling action: This is a fancy term for everything that happens after your climax. Your falling action should show that the conflict is winding down. Don't skimp on this part, and don't rush it—your readers deserve to know just how things get worked through.

Dorothy and the Wizard work out solutions for each of her friends' problems. Then the Wizard tells Dorothy how she can get home to Kansas.

One Author's Writing Process

Chris Crutcher is the author of numerous books for young readers, including *Ironman*, *Staying Fat for Sarah Byrnes*, *Stotan!*, and *Chinese Handcuffs*. In 2000, he was awarded the American Library Association's Margaret A. Edwards Award, honoring his lifetime contribution in writing for teens.

How do you start writing your books?
The best I can say is, I think of a story and then I tell it. I get started by looking at the heart of the story, what it is about, and begin with some action.

How much rewriting do you do?
I do a tremendous amount of rewriting. Because I start with just the seeds of an idea, it means that as things happen in later chapters, I have to go back to earlier chapters to match them up. I also write down everything, and not everything belongs in the story. I do a LOT of rewriting.

Do you ever have a hard time giving up a great idea that doesn't quite fit a story?
Not anymore. I usually know I'll be able to use it somewhere else. The hard part is realizing that it doesn't belong.

> **How do you get over writer's block?**
> I go away from the story and do something physical and let my mind loose.

The End

The end is also called a *conclusion* or a *resolution*. At the end, you need to settle the conflict. Be sure your characters say and do believable things here. Go back to your character sketches and look for clues that may help you create things they do or say to solve the problems in realistic and believable ways. You might also set your ending in the same place as your beginning—this helps your reader feel that the story has come full circle.

> *Dorothy clicks her red shoes together, chanting, "There's no place like home. There's no place like home," and is back in the original setting—her farm in Kansas. Her family and friends, who closely resemble her friends from Oz, surround her. Their comments and loving concern prove to her that there is no place like home.*

Learn to trust your gut if there are places where your writing seems to trudge along or where you find yourself pausing to reread because it just doesn't feel right. If something isn't working for you, it probably isn't going to work for your audience either. When you're ready to share your writing with your select group of readers, you'll find that, more often than not, these uneasy spots are the very places where your readers will also request a revision.

Steps in the Writing Process

The writing process is a series of steps that the writer goes through before his writing is considered finished. Writers sometimes stop writing in the middle of the process, put it away, and then pull it out later to start writing again. Some writers finish an entire piece over the weekend. No matter how long it takes, most writers go through the following steps for each writing piece:

1. Pre-write or freewrite. This can mean writing in your journal or using writing prompts and exercises.
2. Write a first draft.
3. Revise the first draft.
4. Get responses and comments from people who you think will give you helpful feedback (see more about this in the next chapter).
5. Revise it again, based on reader responses you agree with.
6. Check the piece for spelling and grammar mistakes.
7. Decide where the piece might be published and get submission guidelines. (Sometimes this is the first step in the writing process—we'll talk more about this in chapter 8.)
8. Finalize the piece, making sure it fulfills the publisher's guidelines. Make a copy to keep for yourself.
9. Submit your writing to a publisher.
10. Wait for their answer ... and wait ... and wait ...

Time to Go Public!

Phew! You're finally at the point where you feel your story, poem, or play is just right. Guess what? You're still not done. Now it's time to share it with the world! Let others whose opinions you value read it. Although not everyone will like what you have written, that's okay. You can't please everyone, right? But other people's opinions can be very helpful, as you will see in the next chapter. Letting people read your writing, and then listening to their opinions, can be hard, but it *will make you a better writer*. And it's totally up to you whether or not you take their advice. You are the final judge of your writing.

So, whether you're ready to have others read your writing or are ready to submit it to publishers, read on!

Young Author Profile:
Alexandra Franklin

Inspired by her home state's long history of subtle, tragic literature, eighteen-year-old **Alexandra Franklin** won the national 2010 Scholastic Art and Writing Award before leaving Mississippi to attend the University of Alabama to study poetry and creative writing.

Editor, Best Teen Writing 2011

Editor's Introduction

I wanted this job a lot. I was pretty brassy about it too; I can admit that. I had just graduated from high school in Jackson, Mississippi. I was in New York, I was a Portfolio Gold Medalist, and I had this idea that everything I ever wanted was falling into my lap. I spent most of the awards week begging Alex Tapnio to let me be the editor of the next year's *Best Teen Writing* anthology. I sent emails. I was, basically, very annoying.

Exactly one year later, I was in Manhattan again, at dinner with the Alliance staff after the awards ceremony at Carnegie Hall. I had a brand-new name tag with my name above the word *staff* (I took pictures of this and sent it to my parents, who were suitably impressed). "You know what I remember most about you?" Alex said, referring to our encounter in 2010. "You were totally gunning for that editor's job. I mean, you really wanted it."

I really did. I wanted to be involved. I wanted to be the one who got to wade through the manuscripts, meeting the new writers, soaking up the new voices.

I started going through the pool of award-winning writing in March, and I didn't surface for months. My three roommates got used to waking up in the morning to find me already sitting at our kitchen table, fixated on a piece of short fiction or a collection of poetry, my coffee cold and untouched at my elbow. I couldn't tear myself away. I wanted to read everything twice. The vastness of the job revealed itself later, when I had to start narrowing down the manuscripts from the original stack. I had spent hours every day with these exquisite pieces of writing, falling in love over and over. I couldn't imagine selecting only a few pieces. I suggested a multivolume set; the Alliance politely rejected my suggestion. At least I tried.

The writing in this collection represents a few of the strongest voices from 2011's writing award winners. It's a complicated spectrum of stories—shockingly funny, devastating, wry, tragic—but regardless of genre or tone, each individual voice is stunning. These writers handle words with an expert touch that is rare for their age. They are very, very good at their craft, and this is only the beginning. I am immensely honored to have been among the first to read the new literary voices of this generation.

Particularly in a career like writing, you never get anywhere alone. I'd like to first thank the Alliance for Young Artists & Writers for the years of opportunities, encouragement, and affirmation. Thanks to Lisa Feder-Feitel for being such a warm and motherly source of comfort, to Katie Babick and Michael Vinereanu for more than I can list here, to Kerri Schlottman for keeping me on track, and to Alex, Danniel, Nick, John Sigmund, John Kollmer, Nora, Dominic, Kat, and Virginia for making me feel at home and helping me in countless ways every day. Special gratitude goes to Dr. Paul Smith, for being wise, encouraging, and in love with words; and to my family, who has come to accept that maybe this writing thing isn't just a phase. Specifically, thank you to my mother, who helped put together my first book when I was four. (We've come a long way since then, haven't we?) I also owe a lot to Dan, for his infinite patience when I hit the workahol a little too hard, and to Claire, whose chai lattes got me through plenty of days of nonstop reading.

And finally—most significantly—thank you to all of the young writers whose work was under consideration for this anthology. I know your names and your stories, and I have no doubt that I will encounter them again. Let this be the beginning and not the end. Find out what drives you to write, what gets under your skin, what makes writing feel like a compulsion and not a hobby, and chase that inspiration. But even if you decide that you are not, ultimately, a writer, I truly believe that you will each do great things. I can only echo what Rilke writes in *Letters to a Young Poet*: "Your life will still find its own paths from there, and that they may be good, rich, and wide is what I wish for you, more than I can say."

Cheating at Cards
Short Story

I cut myself shaving this morning. I wasn't paying attention, and I let the razor slide sideways, and it opened up a deep, narrow seam in my shin. I didn't even notice it until I stepped out of the shower and the blood ran in diluted pink rivulets between my toes. Now, already, the skin is just beginning to meet and weave together again.

I paid $400 for a roundtrip ticket home. I cannot begin to calculate how far behind I am in paying the rent, but I paid $400 to come home, to sit on the bed I slept in until I was seventeen, and to play gin rummy with Mary Elizabeth. We've been playing cards like this for as long as I can remember, and I don't think either of us knows how to play without cheating.

"I've taken her to doctors," Mary whispers. Our conversation started at normal volume but has gradually slipped until we are inexplicably whispering. Neither of us wants to be the first to speak up. It reminds me of when we were small and staying up too late, holding hands across the gap between our matching twin beds. "I've taken her to doctors and I've even made doctors come here to see her. They all say nothing is wrong."

"If she says she's sick ..." I shuffle the deck flashily, Vegas-style, and pull out ten cards for each of us. I rifle shamelessly through hers before presenting them with a flourish.

"I don't know what to do anymore."

"I'm glad you called me."

Mary sizes me up. "I'll pay you back for the ticket."

"Yeah," I say, humoring her.

"Maybe I should go check on her."

"She's fine, she's asleep." My sister worries too much. "Just sit. Play this hand."

But she's distracted now, her baby-fine, corn-silk hair swaying back and forth over her shoulder. Her narrow body is curved tensely over her lap, and her fingers hover above the cards like a tarot reader's. I remember when I could pull her against me, rub her shoulders, and calm her down. Now I sit and watch her, motionless and dreamlike, only half-invested in this particular scene.

Mary is flipping through cards now without strategy or purpose. She presses two kings together, turns a queen's back on both of them. She spins a jack away from the pile and several mundane subjects—a three of hearts, a seven of clubs—slide haplessly under the bed. I feel terrible for leaving her here to cope with our mother's compulsions. My fingers drift to the cut on my shin. "You're enabling her."

"I'm taking care of her," Mary maintains. She obscures her face with a curtain of hair, but her back stiffens dangerously. When she was eight and I was twelve, I told her what I knew about the legitimacy of the Santa Claus story. I haven't thought about it until now, but I remember that her reaction was the same. Regret tastes salty in my mouth. I always know the right thing to say, but I can never bring myself to say it.

She sighs and collapses onto the pillows, reaching up to turn off the lamp. I push a dozen teddy bears to the floor and curl up beside her. Our hips nearly touch; our fingers are so close I can feel the static between them. The green plastic stars that we stuck to the ceiling ten years ago glow dimly.

"Do you know," Mary slurs sleepily, "that the stars we see are just old light from stars that died centuries ago?"

Within minutes, her breathing becomes deep and long. I slip out of bed and down the hall to our mother's room. The door is ajar. A long, thin slice of light falls across the carpet.

I creep into the room and stand beside her bed. The sheets are tangled and twisted; she is not a silent sleeper like Mary. Instead, she thrashes and groans and cries. Her hair is already damp and curling around her forehead. I can feel the heat rising from her bulky form. I am still stinging from the criticism she offered during dinner—shouldn't I be head editor at the *Tribune* by now? After all the time I've put in? After all the tuition she paid? The truth is that I have forgotten what it would mean to advance a career. Like scuba divers who become disoriented and swim away from the surface when their oxygen is low, I am sure that one day I will advance myself right out of the copyediting cubicle and onto the street.

Something is crawling up my leg. No, down my leg. Jesus! I swear silently, which feels wrong to do in my mother's room, even though I am an adult and she is asleep. I am bleeding, but it takes a moment for me to realize that I have been scratching the razor cut on my leg.

I cannot imagine where my mother keeps the Band-Aids. For a hypochondriac, she keeps her first–aid kit woefully bare. It consists of a bandage for sprains, syrup of ipecac, and a pair of tweezers. I sit on the bathroom counter pressing a fistful of Kleenex to my cut and feeling sorry for myself. When the bleeding has slowed, I rummage through her medicine cabinet. She has stocked it like a drugstore. I pull down dozens of bottles of pills for depression and pain and insomnia. There are no Band-Aids. Wearily, I wrap the sprain bandage around my shin and reach up to the tiny window near the ceiling. It's painted shut, but I force it open and take long drags of the cold air. The lights from the city reflect against the clouds, projecting a smoky cap over the horizon. They drown out the stars that traveled for centuries just to be seen tonight.

At a Dinner Party the Night Before the Divorce Is Finalized
Poetry

In crowded rooms I stand alone,
leaning on my whittled bones.
Their brittle laughter spears me through,
as biting as your cheap cologne.
Last fall we needed something new.
You bought six pints of robin blue;
we painted through a week of nights
and hung red drapes to block the view.
We thought the paint would make it right,
and though we tried, it wasn't quite
enough to seal the growing split
that led us here. You're so polite
and calm. You kill them with your wit.
You're charismatic, I admit—
you charmed me once. God, what a sin;
I once thought I could shrink to fit
your standards. I was lovely then.
Tonight they press my icy skin
and whisper that this poor girl's grown
as hollow as a violin.

7

You've Written Your Masterpiece: Now What? Let Them Read It

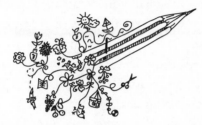

*Y*ou *finally found a way to end your story with something besides
"... and they lived happily ever after." Your setting is full of great
descriptions, and you added some new dialogue. You even ran it through
spell-check. Nothing left to do now but print it out and ... oh no! Horror
of horrors. You have to let a real human being actually read your writing!*

Actually, you don't *have* to let anyone read your writing. Sometimes
it's fun to write something just for yourself, something that no one
else will see. But there's a difference between being a writer and
being a *published* writer. You are a writer as soon as you start writing. But to be a published writer, you will have to let someone else
read and judge your writing. And it *can* be pretty scary to show
your writing to someone else.

So, now's the time to make your decision. You've spent a lot
of time and effort writing something and you feel pretty good
about it. Are you ready to show it to someone you trust? Getting
a reader's opinion is incredibly valuable to you as a writer. Once
your piece is out there—submitted to a publisher, contest, whatever—it's done. It's too late to find out what messages readers will

understand from your writing and whether they will discover your true meaning. Asking someone to read and respond to your writing is a great opportunity to receive valuable feedback *before* you finalize your piece.

What Is a Reader?

A *reader* is someone who will read and respond to your writing—that is, readers will give you their opinions on what they think is good and bad about what you've written. Unfortunately, very few people know how to respond to writing beyond checking the spelling and grammar. Don't you just hate it when you want someone's opinion, but all they do is point out your misspelled words? That's what spell-check is for. But you can bet that most readers will assume spell-checking is all you want them to do, unless you tell them otherwise. Readers who give you feedback about your plot, your characters, your word choices, and so on are much more helpful to your writing.

How to Find a Good Reader

How do you choose someone to read your work? There are two kinds of readers you should consider asking:

1. Readers who represent the people who will actually want to read your piece (otherwise known as your *intended audience*). If you're writing a kid's book, have a kid read it. If you're writing about a teen girl, have a teen girl read it. See if it's believable and enjoyable to them.
2. Readers whose opinions on writing you value.

Both types of readers are extremely valuable to you as a writer, and each can offer you different insights. We're sure you can think of a few good people who will read your writing and give you their responses: teachers, parents, grandparents, aunts, uncles, the local librarian, and of course, your friends.

One tip: Don't ask *too* many people to be your readers. You know the saying "Too many cooks can spoil the soup"? Well, that goes for your writing as well: too many readers can spoil your story. If you get too many opinions, you will have a hard time deciding whom to listen to. Find one or two people you trust and ask them first. Save everyone else for your next stories.

Writing Groups

Joining a writing group can be a fantastic way to grow as a writer. A writing group is just a group of writers who share and comment on each other's writing on a regular basis. You can find a writing group to join by asking teachers and librarians in your area. You can even start your own group! Just find a few friends who like to write and ...

Writing Group Checklist
Here's what you might do if you decide to organize a group yourself:

1. Set up a regular meeting date and time (for example, every Tuesday at 3:30 PM).
2. Set up a regular location (schools, libraries, and local bookstores are often very willing to give you space if you ask, or you can rotate at each other's homes).
3. Assign a leader (or set up a list to take turns) who will:
   * bring one fun writing prompt;
   * keep the group on task;
   * watch the time.
4. Have snacks—a must! They are a great way to stay energized. Take turns being in charge of this crucial task.
5. Use the same meeting agenda each week (see the following page).

Meeting Agenda
Here are the types of things you can do during your meetings:

1. Freewrite (write nonstop on any topic) for ten minutes. Don't worry about spelling, grammar, or complete sentences.
2. Do a read-around of all or part of each freewrite, with no comments (laughing, however, is allowed!).
3. Present a writing prompt and write silently for ten minutes.
4. Do another read-around of parts or wholes, with comments on what was strong or stood out.
5. End the meeting by reading pieces that members brought to share with the group. These are usually pieces that were started in previous sessions but have been revised and finalized. It's nice if the author prints out enough copies for each member.

You can also start or join a writing group online. Gather a group of friends and decide how you'll meet online (Skype, social media, and so on). Or you can find a group that's already online—do a little research to make sure your interests match the group's. Many of the big publishers run online writing groups where your work might even be noticed by an editor!

What to Ask Your Reader

Believe it or not, you will probably have to coach your readers a bit in order to get the helpful responses you're looking for. Before you ask people to read your writing and give you their opinions, know what you want from them. Fill them in on the parts you struggled with and are still worried about. Tell them what you'd like them to look for and what types of suggestions you'd like. Here are some things to say and questions to ask your readers before and after they read your piece:

1. I think I am (still in the early stages/almost finished) writing this piece.
2. I'd really love your ideas on how to improve the beginning of the story (or the setting or a particular character, or whatever you need).
3. Which words, phrases, characters, plot events, and so on stand out to you or seem particularly strong?
4. Which seem particularly weak?
5. Were there any gaps in the plot or characters that need more description?
6. How did the writing make you feel? Did it remind you of anything?
7. Is there anything you would change about the piece?

When you seek the input of readers and trust the feedback coming your way, welcome the praise and the criticisms equally. You don't have to agree with everything your readers are saying, but even disagreement gives strength and conviction to your writing. Remember that you handpicked these readers, so you must respect their opinion for a reason. Give some time and space to their feedback if you find that you're getting emotional or upset about it. Often, we get most bothered when we realize there is some truth to what we're hearing. Your readers just want you to put your best foot forward, so LISTEN TO THEM! After all, you can't become a seasoned writer if you're unwilling to consider—and gracefully accept—the opinions of others.

Fear!

Okay, we all have fear, especially the fear of criticism or rejection. In fact, most writers have an especially hard time with it. Writing can be a very personal experience, and showing your personal thoughts to someone else is not easy. It might help to keep in mind that a reader's opinion is just that—one opinion. There are probably other opinions out there too. It's *your* writing, and you are the one who decides whether to change it or not. If one reader's opinion doesn't work for you, get another one. Remember, your reader is just trying to help, not rip your heart out.

You and your reader should understand that there is no right or wrong way of viewing a piece of writing, just what the reader understood when she read it. Later, you will decide whether you communicated your idea well or whether you need to make any of the suggested changes to help other readers get your point.

What to Do with Reader Comments

Here are some things to keep in mind when sifting through feedback from readers:

1. Remember that this is your writing and any decisions about changes are up to you. Reader comments—you can take 'em or leave 'em, but no matter what, you should think about them.
2. Remember that you asked for their comments and your readers are only trying to help. Always say thank you. They took time out of their busy lives to read and think about your writing. Even if you disagree with their opinions, you should be grateful for their help.
3. Take notes on what your readers said. Did they seem confused? Did they ask questions? Can you answer them by adding to or clarifying your writing? Were they interested in a particular point or character and want to know more about it? Think about what you can add, delete, rearrange, or reword to make sure your future readers get just what you want them to get from your writing.
4. On the computer, save a copy of your story with the word "revised" in the title. Keep your original just as it is. Work on the revised copy and don't touch your original. Save it for later.
5. Start revising. Clarify, add, delete, rearrange—experiment. You can always go back to the original if you're not happy with the revisions.

6. Put the writing away after you have revised it. Come back in a day or two and read it again with fresh eyes. You'll probably be encouraged by your progress and might even be tempted to revise it some more! Don't worry—go ahead and make it even better. We won't tell!

A Self-Made Success Story

Amanda Hocking is nothing if not a success, yet her story is not that of an author taking her manuscript to publisher after publisher before hitting it big. She became her own publisher, selling her first books on Amazon as ebooks. Her website, amandahocking .blogspot.com, gives some details of her success in her own words.

Early Interest Sets the Stage

"My father was a journalist, so I grew up seeing him type to earn a living. His example made writing seem like a normal thing to do.

"People ask me, 'When did you start writing?' And the truth is, I never didn't write. Before I could talk, I would tell stories. When I was younger, I couldn't write fast enough to keep up with the ideas I had, so I had to talk and get them out. When I was twelve, I decided that writers were boring people, and I didn't want to be boring, so I'd save writing for my 'safety' career while I tried out other ones. In high school, I probably wrote about fifty short stories and started a dozen novels.

"I finished my first novel when I was seventeen, right after I graduated high school. I assumed that, once I wrote a book, I would become rich and famous. This is apparently not how things work in the writing world."

Combining Craft and Determination

Hocking went to college but found that the only thing she was interested in was writing, so she dropped out after a semester. She went to work but always kept writing—and getting rejected. Then in November 2008, she said, "This is it. I'm going to get published." She went to the stores and looked at what was selling compared to what she was writing.

"At Walmart, I saw 700 vampire novels. I said to my roommate, 'I like vampires. I'm going to write a vampire novel and that will be my door into publishing. From this, I will be able to launch my career.'" Hocking wrote the vampire novel in fifteen days. "Then for good measure, I wrote another. I edited, revised, edited, revised. I queried. I got rejected."

Hocking discovered she enjoyed writing paranormal romance. And she did her homework on the genre. "I saw *Star Trek* in the theater and came home and wrote *Switched* in a week. (During that time I wrote around nine to fourteen hours a day. I only ate ravioli, Red Bull, and SweeTarts.)" Again she wrote and revised, only to be rejected. But she says she got great advice from some publishers on how to improve her work.

Staying Open to Opportunity

Two years later, Hocking still had not found a publisher. A turning point came when she read a post on Twitter that directed her to an article about Elisa Lorello and her novel *Faking It*. "She made it to the top 100 in Kindle, and she didn't have a publisher," says Hocking. "I didn't think I'd have any kind of success with ebooks, but I kept researching it. Eventually, I decided that even if I only sold a few copies of any book, it'd be better than the pile of rejections I had building up.

"In March, I made *My Blood Approves* available in paperback on Amazon through Lulu. In April, I published it to Kindle. About a week or so later, I published the second book in the series, *Fate*. Here's where the story picks up. The two books combined, I sold forty-five copies in about two weeks. I put out *Flutter* at the end of May. I distinctly remember one day in May, before it came out, I sold thirty-eight books in one day. In May, I sold 624 books and made $362."

Just a month later, another discovery: "I discovered book bloggers. I had no idea such people existed. They just read books and write about them. I asked several if they would be interested in reviewing my books, and most of them said yes, even if they didn't generally review self-published work."

Then her books really started selling. In June of that year, she sold 4,258 copies of her three books combined and made a total of $3,180. Hocking's career has continued to skyrocket and, by 2011, she had sold over a million copies of nine books and earned $2 million from sales—something previously unheard of for self-published authors.

Hocking continues to write, but says, "I've already far surpassed my expectations. I just don't know what's next." Whatever is next for this twenty-six-year-old author, she has clearly proved that if you want to write and be published, keep writing—and keep your eyes peeled for opportunity. The world of publishing changes all the time. Maybe you will join Amanda Hocking and blaze a new trail of publishing success.

Be true to yourself and true to your reader by remembering why you're writing. Do you write for you alone? For an audience? For regular pay? All of the above? Whatever your reason, uphold that purpose by providing the appropriate tools and outlet. Don't get mad or frustrated when you're going in the wrong direction with your creations—like submitting a stream-of-consciousness journal entry to a writing contest! Your voice, your passion, your income—writing can be all of these things, but its greatest potential lies in your ability to recognize the realistic time, place, and means for you to be the best wordsmith you can be within any given purpose.

Congratulations!

You've finished writing something, you've revised it (probably more than once), and you've even shown it to a few people and received feedback from readers. Give yourself a big pat on the back and treat yourself to some chocolate chip cookie dough ice cream—a time-honored tradition among writers! Now it's time to move on to bigger and better things—it's time to share your writing with the world!

Young Author Profile:
Kevin Hong

A native of Needham, Massachusetts, seventeen-year-old **Kevin Hong** was selected as one of 20 U.S. Presidential Scholars in the Arts in 2011 before heading to Harvard College to continue his writing. His influences include Joseph Brodsky, Rainer Maria Rilke, and Jorge Luis Borges.

The Spectrum
Short Story

Shen, the house painter, could see the family inside, in the lighted kitchen, engulfed in the vapors from the huge pot of soup. They seemed very full and happy. The boy, seven or eight years old, occasionally leaned back in his chair to throw out a belch whose volume Shen could gauge from the laughter of his parents on either side, and they would ladle more soup into his bowl and smack their lips at the meat that slid off the bone (he could see steam slip from the bone as well). The room looked hot. It rose in Shen's eyes like a loaf of bread, so when the wife stepped outside and called up to the roof to invite him and his crew in for some turkey soup—so cold today, she said—it was all Shen could do to swallow his saliva and say, "No, thank you. We have food in the van." The wife went in. He pointed his pressure hose at the skylight to blot out his view of the kitchen.

The Harpers' house seemed always to be full of light. The curtains were open during the day, when Mrs. Harper did housework, and sun flooded the windows, washed over shadows like a tide, sunk into the hardwood floors. In the morning, Shen liked to work on the front of the house, the east side, where the sun warmed his back. From that side, he could see the family room and the dining room on the first floor, and Mr. Harper's study and the master bedroom on the second. There was a small balcony just above the front door from which he could see the foyer, the grand staircase leading to the second floor, and a large chandelier. The light hung twelve feet from the floor on a long, gold chain. It looked like a giant crystal bowl and twinkled throughout the day. The living room and the kitchen were on the west side. The sunroom, white with white tiles, abutted the kitchen to the south. Its roof was lower than that of the rest of the house. Sunlight congregated there late morning and into the afternoon, through its glass doors and windows, and through the two skylights on the roof. Shen was standing atop the sunroom now. It was here, by the skylights, that he could observe the Harpers' dinner in the kitchen. He was washing the south wall of the second floor and attic. The pressure hose roared against it, and mist formed a rainbow in the air. Amid the noise, Shen peered down and imagined their conversation, the clatter of dishes and silverware.

At dusk, he descended from the roof. He called out to Bo and Sunny, who shut off the water and began loading the van. Shadows broke over the backyard as the last of the sun touched the west side of the house, which glistened like the surface of a lake. The light in the kitchen grew only brighter. It looked as if the Harpers were swimming in it. Shen walked to the driveway and started the van. Jazz was playing on the radio, and he lit a cigarette while he waited for Bo and Sunny to finish packing up. They were arguing about the Rockets game when they clambered in. They were both young. Bo, a squat, red-faced man, insisted that this was their lucky year. Sunny, dark-skinned and rough, insulted each of the starters, Bo, and then Bo's mother.

"Your arguments have no substance," Bo said. "That's why you're so crude. It's a shield you use to hide your vacuousness."

"Vacuum my ass," Sunny said. "Slob. Go stuff your face with a watermelon."

Shen said nothing. He put the van in gear and pulled out of the driveway.

Shen had looked at Mr. Harper with surprise at their first meeting, when the man, tall and barrel-chested and with the ruddy beard of a poet, said, "We'll be keeping the same color, the peach." He hadn't even glanced at the color scheme. Shen looked up from it, and Mr. Harper was staring at him, as if daring him to make a snide remark. But the house painter knew little English, and instead had shaken the husband's hand. They smiled at each other. Shen tried to make his eyes say "Women" with a sly, knowing twinkle, and Mr. Harper responded with a shrug, as if he had long ago yielded control over his own aesthetic to his wife. Shen had never married, but he had been in love, once.

In any case, Shen discovered that he liked the peach paint. It wasn't too bright, and it contrasted nicely with the evergreen and maple flanking the house. At sunset, from the driveway, the house seemed to glow with the kind of energy that old temples give off, that resonates long after the mosaics have chipped and the walls have cracked.

After the day of power washing, Shen and his crew began to scrape. They laid blue canvas and bedspreads over the bushes and small trees surrounding the house, and then, in the late morning, climbed their ladders armed with putty knives and heat guns. From up high, the house felt like a huge boat surrounded by water, and up on the scaffolds, they were like sailors in the crow's nests. Mr. Harper had gone off to work, and the boy was at school. With the gun, Shen loosened old paint from the wall and then slid his knife into the pockets of air and peeled. When he stepped down from his ladder for a smoke, he glimpsed Mrs. Harper in the living room. He was on the east side, but through the opening in the wall of the family room, he could make out her figure, poised over a low table covered with a mound of clothes.

She could have been a dancer, judging by her motions. She was tall and slender, with long legs and a graceful neck. She wore her hair in a ponytail that whipped from shoulder to shoulder as she worked. It was dark brown, but when sunlight caught it, refracted through its wisps, her hair turned red, nearly the color of the Japanese maple in the front yard. Shen walked by the living room windows during the crew's lunch break. It was hard to see inside the house because of the way the sun, just past its zenith, glanced off the glass, but he could discern Mrs. Harper's silhouette, now bending, now lifting the hamper, now propping it on her hip. Each form melted into the next. He watched her glide from the living room toward the stairs as if the floor were covered with ice.

The Harpers' cat also roamed the house. He was orange with yellow stripes, and he liked to prowl up and down the stairs. Once in a while, on his patrol, he would stop at the top and look at the chandelier. His head would tilt to one side, hinged on some vertebra between mild curiosity and keen interest, and his tail would swing in a slow arc, as if he were calculating the velocity of some invisible pendulum, some unseen momentum of the chandelier.

All of the flaking paint had been scraped away by lunch. In the afternoon, the crew used electric sanders to feather the clapboards. Shen ignored the incessant grinding; he focused instead on the flurries of dust that rose into the sun's scope and then floated to the ground or were dispersed by a breeze. Some of it swirled around his arms and head and shined, shot through with light. He felt as if he were inside a snow globe. He sanded with his right hand, and with his left he could feel tremors running through the wall, could imagine the sound shaking the rooms inside.

He was on the balcony in the early afternoon when Mrs. Harper was sweeping the foyer. She moved backward toward the stairs, her steps light and delicate, and bowed down with broom and dustpan as if coaxing some intangible force toward her. When she reached the stairs, she turned and started up, straightening her back. Then, suddenly—it must have been a rush of blood, Shen thought—she swayed to the side and caught herself on the railing. She rested the broom and dustpan beside her and rubbed her eyes. Shen saw her insert a pinky into her left ear, as if it were waterlogged or had an itch. She stayed there for half a minute, slouched, breathing slowly. Then, continuing up the stairs, she looked to her left and saw Shen.

He had stopped working. The balcony creaked as he started and shifted his weight, realizing where he was, what he was doing. His electric sander was still on, whining, running against air. Mrs. Harper looked annoyed, or maybe just surprised; her brow was furrowed and her mouth was slightly open, her nostrils flared. She must have felt uneasy at least. Bits of sun had spun themselves into her hair.

Shen broke first; he gave a little smile and then moved out of the window's frame and began sanding again. His right hand was numb from the machine's vibrations. After a minute, he couldn't help but glance back inside. Mrs. Harper was going back down the stairs, broom and dustpan in hand again, sweeping each step. When she reached the bottom, she crossed the foyer and entered the kitchen, probably for a glass of water. A moment later, the cat appeared on the stairs, and Shen followed it down as well.

The cat, he'd noticed, moved slowly and kept low, as if searching for a purpose. Maybe he thought he would happen upon one, catch it scurrying toward a mouse hole or a crack in the wall. After lunch, Shen had caught sight of the cat swiping at the galaxies that Mrs. Harper beat from the family room curtains. He turned around and around as dust eddied in the air. Shen was about to name the cat Curly, for his dexterous tail, or Li Po—the cat was certainly a thinker, a poet, and probably a drunk—when the creature, in the midst of a universe of particles, suddenly pounced at Mrs. Harper, hackles up. He opened his mouth and showed her his teeth. Mrs. Harper stepped toward him brandishing her duster, and he—Li Po, Shen finally decided— ducked through her legs and dashed up the stairs.

Late that day Shen saw Mrs. Harper again, in the master bedroom. He was on his ladder at the southeast corner of the house. She had drawn the curtains, but they were thin, and he could make her out, sprawled face-up on the king bed. He turned off the electric sander so she would not be disturbed, and the stirring of leaves in the trees filled him.

Li Po trotted in and leaped to Mrs. Harper's side; he nuzzled her as if to make amends, and she stroked his neck and behind his ears. She reached behind her head to undo her ponytail, and her hair spilled onto the pillow. Li Po nestled on her belly. They looked very peaceful together and lay there until the school bus squealed. Then Mrs. Harper started, sat straight up. The cat toppled from her body and slinked away. Shen turned from the window to see the yellow bus at the end of the driveway and the Harpers' little boy emerging from it, his book bag jouncing. The boy stopped at the mailbox to retrieve the day's mail and then ran toward the house, his arms laden. Shen looked back into the bedroom, but the woman was gone.

Below, the front door opened, and Mrs. Harper met her son outside. The boy dropped the mail onto the ground as she knelt and kissed his cheek. When he pressed his face into his mother's chest and reached his arms up around her neck, her hair fell about his head like a private forest. She was murmuring something into his ear, and he was giggling. Then Mrs. Harper stood, and the boy scampered about, picking up the envelopes and magazines that had scattered on the ground. He said something about a Mrs. Patterson—Mrs. Patterson had read them a story about a hippo, and they were learning how to write lowercase letters in cursive. Shen did not understand.

The boy collected the last piece of mail and went inside the house, and his mother followed. She looked up just before she closed the door, looked up and to the left at Shen on his perch.

Shen pretended to be inspecting the window frames. Then the door shut. He suddenly felt dizzy. He stepped down from the ladder and ambled to the driveway for a smoke.

After the sanding, they washed the house again. The paint that remained on the walls was dull, de-glossed. The house looked old and mottled, as if it had risen from the earth. But the family inside, at dinner that evening, looked as cheerful as ever. From the roof of the sunroom, Shen saw Mrs. Harper lean her head against her husband's shoulder as he served vegetables, saw his arm around her. Their son's face was as round and as bright as a porcelain doll's. Mr. Harper tousled his hair, and then they fell to eating. As shadows consumed the backyard, the kitchen's light stayed strong. It bloomed into the dark. Shen shut off his hose and called out to Bo and Sunny. They began loading the van.

They waited a day for the house to dry and then began to apply the primer. Sunny and Bo started at opposite ends of the west wall and worked toward the middle, while Shen worked alone on the east side. The stuff smelled strongly, as if demanding his attention. There were three days of painting—one for the primer and two for the finish. He worked patiently, slowly, as he covered the clapboards; there was no rush, and he did not want to get tired.

He began at the upper-left corner of the wall. He painted from left to right until the entire level was done, and then moved down a few rungs on his ladder. Again and again he climbed down the ladder, repositioned it, and climbed back up. When he finally did feel weary, he turned around and lay back on the ladder's rungs. He breathed deeply and closed his eyes or squinted into the sun. These moments, he felt almost completely detached from the earth. Only a few metal bars held him up from the ground thirty feet below.

During lunch, the crew sat around a crockpot of rice and a foil container full of pork cuts. Bo produced an embroidered handkerchief from his pocket and wiped sweat from his face.

"Have you met someone?" Sunny asked.

Bo grinned. "No kidding," Sunny said.

Bo wrinkled his nose. "But this paint," he said. "What a caustic stench! I think I'm going stupid."

"Too late," Sunny said, and laughed.

"Seriously," Bo said, "my eyes feel swollen. I feel like there's a probe poking around in my nose. I think I'm developing a condition."

Shen smiled to himself; Bo and Sunny were young and inexperienced. He didn't mind the paint so much. He had never really minded uncomfortable sensations; he had learned to shut them out. He remembered a time long ago, in elementary school, when all the students went out during recess with buckets of feces to fertilize the garden in the square. Pairs of students walked through the furrows, one ahead of the other, sharing the load of a bucket that swung from the middle of a pole resting on their shoulders. The furrows were like balance beams; they were careful not to fall over. Sometimes they sang, and the melodies floated from their mouths and over their heads like wisps of smoke. Shen remembered this as he watched Sunny and Bo go back and forth. He wanted to tell the two of them what he was thinking, but he left it alone.

"You get used to it" was all he said. Then he stood up and returned to work.

But he found himself dozing off in the afternoon. The paint, or maybe the sun, dulled his senses to the point where he swayed on the ladder, half-asleep. His ears felt stuffed; he suddenly wanted to drop everything, his paintbrush, his heavy bucket. He wouldn't have cared if the paint splashed against the canvas on the ground, splattered on the lawn and the walkway and the front steps. He got down from the scaffold and, rubbing his temples, shuffled down the driveway. He leaned against the van and tried to take in some fresh air, but it was no use. He lit a cigarette. His head kept buzzing. Then he saw the school bus lurching down the street. It pulled up in front of him and belched its exhaust. Shen straightened, dropped his cigarette, and smashed it under his heel. The door of the bus opened and the Harpers' little boy hopped out. He was wearing a blue jacket with a big hood drawn over his head. His brown hair framed his eyes and pale cheeks. He looked up at Shen and squinted, until Shen stepped forward and his shadow fell upon the boy like a cloak. He must have looked like a giant silhouette against the sun. He remembered the first time he had seen a deer—how, at his slightest movement, the creature caught wind and ran away. He felt slow and awkward in front of the boy.

"What's your name?" he asked. His voice was raspy.

"Joel," the boy said. He blinked and looked down at Shen's feet and up again. His eyes were light gray, almost translucent. He was missing one of his front teeth. "What's yours?"

"Shen."

Joel Harper put out his right hand. Shen took it gingerly in his. He felt like a child in the boy's eyes.

"That's a funny name," Joel said. "Where did you get it?"

"From my parents," Shen said. "From China."

"China!" Joel said. "What's China like?"

Shen opened his mouth to speak and then faltered. "What's it like?" he said.

Joel nodded.

He did not know how to answer the question. What did the boy want to know? Would he understand if Shen tried to explain customs, cultures, and histories that were entirely foreign to him? Had the boy any perception of distance and time? What did he know of hills like giant hands, terraced fields, sun spreading on land and lake like a copper mirror?

"Very big," Shen said. The rest of it he held under his tongue.

"How far away?" Joel said.

Shen thought again. "Very far."

His arm felt rusty in its socket, but he lifted it and gestured toward the west. He made a throwing motion, as if he had a spear in his hand and he could follow its arc. Joel followed it with him.

"I'm going to travel around the world someday," the boy said. "I'm going to be an explorer." He took a step toward the mailbox.

"Good," Shen said, "very good." His English was loud and abrupt. His heart was caught in his throat.

"But I wouldn't want to go fast," Joel said. "I wouldn't want to go around the world in eighty days. I want to see everything! I'd want to go around the world in"—he scratched his head, and his hood slipped off—"ten hundred years."

Sunlight set off his hair, which took on the same red hue as his mother's. He opened the mailbox and peered inside, and then, with both hands, brought out a large envelope and several magazines and letters. The envelope was almost as big as his torso. Shen thought he could have scooped him up with one arm and lifted him onto his shoulders. Joel smiled and stepped past him on the driveway.

"Nice meeting you," the boy said, glancing back. "Bye."

"Yes, good," Shen said, as Joel walked away. "Goodbye."

The boy clutched the mail to his chest as he trundled up to the house. On cue, the front door opened, and Mrs. Harper stepped outside. Joel ran into her outstretched arms. Shen saw her look down the driveway at him and thought he saw a frown. Then they were inside, the door shut. Shen blinked at the sun, stretched his arms, and walked slowly back. He climbed his ladder and resumed work. The primer stung his nostrils, but he welcomed it. He moved his brush in a long, simple phrase.

At dusk, he sat by one of the skylights on the roof of the sunroom. Sunny and Bo were finishing the north side of the house. Sunny was making fun of one of Bo's few and fleeting conquests, and Bo's protests fluttered through the air. The house smelled of vitriol, but the roof received occasional breezes that filled the trees. Shen breathed deeply and looked at the clouds smoldering from the setting sun.

He lay back, and his mind's magician flung his cards out in the sky. Shen surveyed them as a feudal lord surveys his many acres.

Closer, Joel's face, scrunched, looking into the sun. Beyond that, the boy stooping to pick up a piece of mail from the ground. Then Shen recalled his collection of cigarette cartons, which, in his youth, were tradable items—Golden Gate, Triple Happiness, Lucky Red. His father, barefoot on the cement of the kitchen floor, running in place to keep warm. His brother gnawing on a stale rice cake. Chi Li, the ladies' man, burning the sky on his motorcycle, the only motorcycle in town, colorful streamers flowing from the handlebars. The exhaust, a shooting star.

He saw a woman sitting up in bed, combing her long, black hair, both straps of her nightgown loose about her arms. One slender leg slipped out from under the sheets and dangled over the side of the bed; her foot arched toward the ground, perfectly pointed, as if poised to enter a body of water. Shen turned and looked down through the skylight into the Harpers' kitchen.

They were seated around the table as usual. Mr. Harper was carving a roasted chicken. Mrs. Harper was ladling soup. Joel blew on the soup in his bowl and watched the steam that rose and wove itself into latticework. What did the boy see? A bridge, maybe, or a pair of trapeze artists in a circus act, a tower—and then Shen noticed that the boy was looking at him. He froze, afraid that Joel had spotted him, but realized in a moment that the boy could see nothing beyond the skylight; it was too dark outside. Nevertheless, Shen climbed down from the roof, careful not to make any noise, and smoked a cigarette in the driveway. He waited in the van for Bo and Sunny to finish painting. When they were done, they loaded the van. In the rearview mirror, as Shen steered away, the sun's last light gilded the house.

The work continued on schedule. The crew began applying the first finish. Shen noted as he climbed his ladder that the leaves were changing. The trees that bordered South Street branched out toward each other, forming a natural arbor or columned passageway that was tinged with red and yellow.

On their break, mid-morning, Bo recited poetry. They smoked in a circle by the van, and Bo waved his cigarette in the air, creating skinny rivers, curling shapes. He never really inhaled on the cigarette; he just liked to hold it. He was especially fond of the ancient poet Du Fu:

"The trees shed leaves that rustle, rustle down,

And endlessly, the river surges, surges on.

A guest of autumn's sorrow, of ten thousand miles,

Of a hundred years of ills, I climb the terrace alone."

Sunny laughed at him. "A poet now, eh?" he said. "No wonder the ladies are so hot for you."

"Don't make fun of poetry just because you can't understand it," Bo said.

"Du Fu, tofu," Sunny said. "Get over yourself. I can live without that sentimental crap, thank you very much."

"What do you think, boss?" Bo said.

Shen took a long drag and let the smoke out slowly. It rolled up his face like a thin veil. He didn't really understand the ancient poets, but Bo looked very earnest. Cigarette ash crumbled onto Bo's left boot.

"I guess it's nice," Shen said, and smiled. He stubbed his cigarette as Bo raised his fist in triumph. Sunny snorted and headed back to work.

It was Saturday, and the Harpers were all home. Mr. Harper had spent much of the morning surrounded by his books. As he painted the east wall, Shen had seen him in his study, which was papered with a colorful array of sticky notes that he arranged and rearranged in columns. They were lesson plans, maybe, or story lines. Mr. Harper was a teacher, Shen knew. He had said so when they met. He taught English at the university. The walls of his study were lined with hundreds of books. Shen wondered how old it smelled, how the scent of dog-eared paper filled the room.

Downstairs, Joel was putting together a puzzle in the family room while Mrs. Harper lay on the couch, flipping through the pages of a magazine. Joel looked frail and pretty, unlike his father, but Shen noted with amusement the similarity of their actions. He could watch Mr. Harper organize his notes in different orders, and then work down the ladder to see his son finding a piece that fit, the head of a giraffe or a zebra's tail. Li Po, the cat, meandered up and down the stairs, dividing his time between the two rooms. Mr. Harper let him rest in his lap without breaking concentration; Joel, when Li Po jumped onto the coffee table and stepped on the puzzle, gathered him up in his arms and buried his face in the fur.

In the afternoon, Shen moved to the roof of the sunroom to paint the south wall. Sunny was below, painting the wall of the first floor. The day was at its crest, and Shen felt as tall as the trees, whistled as they did when the wind bustled by. Looking up at the tips of the branches, he felt more than human, or maybe less, like pure air.

The feeling reminded Shen of a place he had visited in his youth, a mountain spring. The water there was pure, and the trees all around were flushed with sun. Gold dappled the ground. A very old man had set up a business there selling prayer flags and blessings, five yuan each, to those who came to drink the water of the spring. For an extra five, one could drink from his gnarled hands. Shen told this to Sunny, who, taking a break, had climbed to the top of his ladder and propped his arms on the roof to listen. He laughed when Shen told him about the hands, and Shen did too. He felt good; he painted as he talked, freely and smoothly, using the entire length of his arm. Then he heard a sound from inside the house. It was almost imperceptible—a dull clatter, like the far-off clapping of wooden chimes.

Shen put his hand up; Sunny had heard it too. The young man climbed up to the roof and crawled to one of the skylights. He peered in and let out a grunt.

"It's the boy," he said. "He's broken a plate."

Shen laid down his brush and joined Sunny by the skylight. Noodles and shards of ceramic were strewn across the kitchen tiles. The nucleus of the mess was at Joel's feet, which were splattered with red sauce. Mr. Harper was there, full-blooded.

Mrs. Harper was on one knee, her arms wrapped around her son, her cheek pressed against his. The man was yelling, but his voice was muffled through the window. He jabbed his index finger at Joel and at the floor. Joel's mother shouted back and held the boy tighter. The man kicked a fragment of the plate and left the kitchen.

Sunny chuckled. "Brings back memories, huh?" he said.

Shen didn't answer. He watched Mrs. Harper dry the boy's tears—which had given his face some color, a hint of pink—and the two of them cleaned up. Joel would not let go of his mother's hand; he held on to it as he bent to pick up shards of the plate. His mother swept the noodles with a broom. Li Po walked among the mess. He sniffed daintily at a meatball and then turned his head with disgust.

"What a baby," Sunny said. "Times sure have changed. A prime example of the decadence of society, as Bo would put it." He crawled back to his ladder, stepped down, and resumed painting the south wall.

Shen remained watching Joel and his mother as they disposed of the mess. Then Joel left the kitchen for the family room while Mrs. Harper turned to the sink. She bowed her head, filled a pot halfway with water, and restarted the stove. Shen held his breath as she leaned over the marble countertop, her hair spread out across her shoulders, and then let it out slowly, steadily. The sounds of cars passing on the road and the wind rolling into the trees came back to him. They carried him back to his work.

The crew finished on Sunday evening. Sunny and Bo began rolling up the canvas and sheets around the house. Shen breathed better, now that the trees and bushes were once again thrown open to the air. They were shadowy in the dim light, like gargoyles on silent guard. Mr. Harper came outside to inspect the work; he started at the driveway, walked around the house, and then returned, nodding to himself. The house, shining with new energy, cut into the sky.

Shen watched Mr. Harper from a few paces away. The man stood tall in the driveway in a T-shirt and shorts. He seemed oblivious to the evening chill. Shen felt angry after what he had witnessed the previous day. It occurred to him, for a moment, that he could speak his mind. Or he could show the man how he felt with merely a word or two, a dismissal, a cold shoulder. He wouldn't, though. Strangely, watching, he admired Mr. Harper, not only for the way he put his hands in his pockets, brows knit in concentration, and let the spirit of the house fill him—he was its patron and its owner, even if he disagreed with its color—but also for the way he seemed to understand matters without knowing anything about them, in the way he cast his eye over the detail of the window frames, could see past the finish to the primer and the sanding, to the power wash of the first day, even though it was dim out, even though he really couldn't see much.

"It looks great," Mr. Harper said. "Really fine." He put his hands together—hands like slabs of meat—and rubbed them. He looked at Shen and smiled through his dense beard. His eyes twinkled, and the painter remembered the joke that they had shared together at the start and wondered if Mr. Harper remembered. Feeling ashamed, Shen merely nodded and looked away.

Then, from the driveway, they heard the storm door swing open. Joel's shout rang out like a shrill violin.

"Bunker's on the chandelier!"

Shen's first reaction was confusion. He did not know what a bunker was. He saw that Mr. Harper was equally as surprised and bewildered; his mouth opened but emitted no sound as he stumbled toward the house. Joel held the door. Mr. Harper ran inside and stopped in the foyer. Shen could see him looking up, hands outstretched, swaying as if he were under a fly ball. Then he realized, and suddenly felt as if he had known it all along, as if the fact had always been with him and had resurfaced at its calling: Bunker was Li Po. Bunker was the cat. The cat had jumped onto the chandelier.

Bo had been carrying a stepladder to the van when Joel shouted. Now Shen took the ladder from him and shouldered it. He went as quickly as he could to the door; seeing him, Joel opened it, saying nothing, only staring, distressed, and Shen angled the ladder through. Mrs. Harper was at the top of the staircase, leaning over the banister toward the chandelier, which was jerking to and fro. Crystals were being knocked loose from it by the four legs that had fallen between the fixture's rings and were each scrabbling for a foothold. Several crystals had already exploded on the ground; Mr. Harper was trying to catch the others before they shattered.

Shen unfolded the ladder and climbed up. He averted his eyes from the light that was intensified by the glass prisms. The three members of the house were shouting over each other—"Watch your feet, Joel!" "Hannah, come down!" "That's glass on the floor!" "Bunker, stop kicking!"—but as Shen reached the top of the ladder, they drew together at the bottom of the stairs and squinted up at the painter. Shen's head was above the light now, and he could see into the bowl of concentric rings, the cat squirming there, and through the rings, he could see the floor lit with stars.

"Watch out!" Joel said. "He doesn't like strangers!"

Bunker yowled as Shen reached into the chandelier and lifted him. The cat twisted and kicked against Shen's chest. Shen could feel the cat's muscles churning, his spine's incredible torque. In his right arm, the body felt almost liquid, like marbles rolling over and over each other. He held the cat tightly against him as he stepped down the ladder. As soon as both of his feet were on the foyer floor, the cat sprang off into the kitchen. Joel hollered and ran after him. The painter straightened and adjusted his coat, which had been perforated by the cat's claws, and then he felt his heart pounding, felt blood pump in every part of his body. He saw Mrs. Harper slip her arm through her husband's. She gave Shen a funny look. He was startled to be so close to her. She was probably remembering the balcony window. And maybe, from inside, she had seen Joel talking with him. Her hair was crimson in the light and her skin was pale.

"Thank you," Mr. Harper said. "I mean, sorry, and thank you."

"No, no," Shen said. He scratched his head and felt paint chips. It was very bright in the foyer. The chandelier was still swinging; the crystals' spectral fragments met the glass that had spread across the floor. The Harpers remained staring at him, as if they expected him to do something, to make a joke or take a bow.

"Yes," Mrs. Harper said, looking down, "yes—thanks." She scuffed a slippered foot against the floor and cleared away a constellation of glass.

Joel came back with Bunker in his arms and elbowed his way in between his parents. He was grinning.

"He's from China!" Joel called out, his voice full of awe.

Mr. Harper laughed. "Oh, is that right? How do you know?"

"He told me!" Joel said. "His name is Shen, and he's from China."

Shen saw Mrs. Harper frown.

"Looks like you've made a new friend," Mr. Harper said.

"How big is China, Dad?"

"How big?" Mr. Harper said. "How big? Let's see. You know my library?"

"Yes."

"There are many books in that library, right?"

"Right!"

"Well," he said, kneeling down, "if you took every single book in that library, and you counted every single word—no, every single letter in every single book—you wouldn't reach half the number of people that live in China."

Joel's mouth fell open. The Harpers looked to Shen for verification. Shen nodded dumbly. The room was moving with colors. The shadows of the Harpers, the railing, the flower vase by the stairs lunged to and fro.

"Well, say goodbye to Shen now," Mr. Harper said to Joel. "He's very tired. He's had a long day."

"Bye," Joel said, as Mrs. Harper stepped behind the boy and put her hands on his shoulders.

Shen pressed down on the bottom step of the ladder to fold it up. He shouldered it as Mr. Harper held the door open.

"Thanks again," the man said, and they shook hands. Then Shen walked out. It was dark outside after the brightness of the foyer. Shadows were thin and long on the front yard. He heard the door shut behind him. Bo and Sunny were waiting in the driveway. He gave them the ladder to secure to the top of the van, and he climbed into the driver's seat.

He switched the engine on and then the heat. Jazz was playing on the radio, the same station as always. Shen did not know the names of the songs or the players, but he could pick up on colors in the sounds that splashed through the van. The saxophone and the cymbals were an orange—acrid but still sweet—that shocked the stretched canvas of air. Bo and Sunny climbed in. Shen pulled down on the gearshift and the van responded like a bull, yoked. He turned right out of the driveway, and the house crossed the length of the rearview mirror. Light burgeoned, soft and gold, from the skylights on the roof of the sunroom where he had worked and rested and watched.

For a mile or so, in his mind he picked his way through the house as if he were exploring an ancient ruin. He saw the boy's muddy shoes just inside the door, a bed of sunlight by the balcony window, the cat's sides rising and falling as he breathed into a weightless sleep. A wonderland of dust, Mrs. Harper's hair spilling down like a cataract, blankets thrown clear of a bad dream. He smelled clean clothes, breathed in a vase of purple flowers. Each sign of life—a curtain moving, a door ajar—seemed to open some reservoir of memory, still full, huge, and silent except for drops of water, condensed on the ceiling, that fell into the pool, echoing. He wondered what had gone through Mrs. Harper's head when she had seen him staring through the balcony window. Why she had stumbled so on the stairs, almost swooned. And what had Joel thought of him as he stood in the driveway in his heavy boots, eclipsing the sun? How had Mr. Harper judged him after inspecting the work, and after Shen had rescued the cat from the chandelier?

It was no wonder to him how the cat had gotten there. Shen could see him at his regular perch at the top of the stairs. He could see him stretch out like an accordion and vault onto the banister and then, with another fearsome leap, reach for the bowl of light. It was less a reach than it was a return, as if the cat had been attached to an invisible, elastic cord, had pulled back as far as he could and then rebounded. Shen saw the crystals again, tripped like a minefield, betraying for a moment all their brilliance. He blinked and the colors were still in his eyes.

"So, what was that anyway, boss?" Sunny called out from the back over the music.

"Nothing," Shen said. "Their cat was stuck."

Sunny and Bo laughed. "I'm going to miss them," Sunny said. "Especially that little crybaby. Some entertainment during the long hours."

"Oh, like you never shed a tear when you were a child," Bo said.

"I never said I didn't. Difference is, my father beat them out of me."

"Maybe that's why you've got such a cold exterior," Bo said. "You've got issues. The thing about the past is, it'll keep growing and growing, and one day it's all you'll have left."

"Shut up," Sunny said. "It's you who keeps growing. Lose some weight, why don't you? The beers can't keep up. Speaking of which ..."

Shen stayed quiet as the two men talked. He drove slowly; the van's headlights illuminated only the immediate road. He rolled down his window to feel the air and heard the trees that arched overhead. He felt as if he were going through a long, winding tunnel. The car was a spirit level, very small and even and centered. Night dragged like a woolen train. Shen reminded himself to send the Harpers' bill and stepped down from the remains of the roof. Pressing the pedal, he felt the engine stir underfoot.

How to Get Published: Creating a Proposal

*T*he alarm goes off and you bury your head deeper under the covers . . . until you remember TODAY IS THE DAY! You are finally going to show the world your writing. Three drafts and three critiques later, you know you have a masterpiece. But how do you get it into people's hands—beyond those people you know personally?

So, you've got that final piece of writing in perfect shape, your readers are responding to it the way you want them to, and you're ready to send it out . . . but where to? A big part of being a writer is (dare we say it?) doing your HOMEWORK! Different magazines and book publishers look for different kinds of writing. You want

Let your writing speak for itself. You don't need fancy packaging or a gimmick to get an editor to notice your submission. In fact, elaborate packaging, like a decorated box or scented paper, might make an editor think you're trying to compensate for a shoddy submission.

to make sure that the person you send your *manuscript* (your written novel, essay, collection, and so on) to is the right one to read it. This doesn't guarantee that the magazine or publishing house will snap it up and instantly publish it, but at least you'll know you've got your foot stuck in the right door.

Steps to Getting Published

Step 1: Figure Out Your Market

The first step in getting published is figuring out the best market for your material. And no, we don't mean go to the grocery store! *Market* is a term magazines and book publishers use to describe the kinds of people who will buy a particular book. For example, if you read only nonfiction history books, you probably won't be *in the market* for a romance novel! Most editors say the worst sin new writers make is sending them writing that isn't appropriate for the market they publish for. That may sound complicated, but it's not. If you have a great nonfiction piece, don't send it to a publishing house that only does fiction books! *That* sounds pretty simple, doesn't it? But you wouldn't believe how many writers don't think about where they send their manuscripts—they just throw 'em out there and hope for the best!

So, how do you find the right market for your writing? Well, you already know which genre your work falls into (you did read chapter 3, right?). Next, decide whom you wrote it for—who's your *intended audience*? Is it young kids? Is it teenagers? Is it all ages? Once you've got those two things figured out, it's time to start searching for the magazine or book publisher who publishes that genre for that market.

Your librarian and English teacher are great people to go to for information and help. You'll find many companies out there that actually specialize in publishing the writing of young people like you! Check out our list in the back of this book. A good place to begin your search is at your local library, with a reference book called *Literary Market Place* (or "the LMP" for those in the know).

This huge book—which is not checked out but used in the library—gets updated every year, weighs about fifteen pounds, and includes the names and addresses of most publishers in the world, plus tons of magazines and contests. Each listing describes the genres that company publishes and the markets they publish for.

Another great way to figure out your market is to go to your local bookstore to find books that you think are similar to your masterpiece. Make a list of the companies who publish these books (you'll find the information in the front of the book on the copyright page, usually the second or fourth page in the book). If you think a magazine is better for your writing, do the same thing in the magazine racks. Most magazine and book publishers also have websites you can visit, which will tell you more about the books and articles they do. Sometimes you can even request a catalogue be sent to you, right over the internet—for free. If you find some book publishers and magazines that have already published your type of writing, they're the most likely to publish that type of writing again, right? You've figured out that your markets match. Way to go!

Step 2: Get the Guidelines

Okay, so you've found a bunch of magazines and book publishers that you think might be interested in your work, based on the kinds of material they publish. Narrow down your choices to five to fifteen places—and you need to be able to keep track of where you send everything. Before you send anything to anyone, however, *get their writer's guidelines!* Writer's guidelines are a checklist of what a magazine or book publisher is looking for and how they like to receive *submissions*. Most publishers make their guidelines available on their website. Some companies will want to see your whole manuscript, while others will just want to see an outline and maybe a short writing sample. All the companies will send you their writer's guidelines for free—all you have to do is call them and ask or check their websites. This step is incredibly important—if you send a magazine or book publisher your writing, but

Sample Publisher's Submission Guidelines

At Beyond Words, we're looking for cutting-edge nonfiction books in the genre of Body, Mind & Spirit. Please note that we are unable to respond to unsolicited email, telephone, and fax queries.

We ARE accepting submissions in Children's, Young Adult, and Adult nonfiction for:
- Body, Mind & Spirit—Material that fosters total well-being in all aspects of a person's life
- Global Native Wisdom—Work that represents the wisdom, traditions, and spiritual viewpoints of indigenous cultures from around the world
- Holistic Health—Guidance from doctors or other medical professionals that integrates the body, mind, and spirit into medical issues
- Science & Spirituality—Investigations into the emerging realms of science
- Spiritual Lifestyles—Books that reflect the changing balance between spirituality and the modern world
- Spiritual Parenting—Thoughtful works for raising and educating spiritual children

We are NOT accepting queries in the following categories:
- Children's and Young Adult picture books, including Poetry/Rhyme
- Fiction, Short Stories, Memoirs, Poetry, or Novels
- Cookbooks, Textbooks, or other Reference books
- Illustrated Coffee Table or Photography books

Please send the entire manuscript if it's complete. If you have a partial manuscript, please indicate its current status in your letter. Whether partial or complete, your query letter should also include the current word count.

A complete proposal MUST contain the following:
- A one- or two-page query letter
- An author biography, including any promotional activities, websites, or marketing items he or she may already be involved with
- At least five sample chapters or the entire manuscript
- A complete synopsis of the book, plus the table of contents
- Market analysis, including comparative/competitive titles already out as well as the book's intended audience
- A self-addressed, stamped envelope (SASE) if you want your materials returned (THERE WILL BE NO RETURNS OTHERWISE)
- All materials must be submitted double-spaced, in 12-point font, and on white 8 1/2 x 11 paper. Please limit your collateral or unusual packaging to the minimum needed to express your point, and always include a SASE (self-addressed, stamped envelope) with sufficient U.S. postage to cover the return of the materials, if desired. If you would not need your materials returned, please state this on your query letter, and let us know whether your submission is simultaneous or exclusive.

Please send submissions to:
Beyond Words Publishing c/o Submissions Department
20827 NW Cornell Road, Suite 500
Hillsboro, OR 97124
Visit the website for updated information and frequently asked questions.

don't follow their writer's guidelines, they're more likely to reject your work. And that's the last thing you want, right?

You will find that some publishers don't accept unsolicited manuscripts, which means they only read material that comes to them through agents. If you do end up looking for one, you will follow the same process and get their guidelines before submitting your work for consideration.

Step 3: Manuscript or Query?

When you get your writer's guidelines, they will tell you to send either a completed *manuscript* or a *query*. Manuscript? Query? What the heck are those? Again, strange words, but simple meanings. A manuscript is what magazines and book publishers call your piece of writing. If they tell you to send your manuscript, that means you should send your entire poem, story, book, whatever, for them to read.

A query is more of a teaser. If they tell you to send a query or query letter, that means they want you to send them just a description of what you've written. They don't want to read your actual writing unless they're interested in the idea. If they like the idea in your query, then they'll ask you to send the entire manuscript later.

Make sure you send exactly what they ask for. If a book publisher wants to see a query, don't send a manuscript. If a magazine wants to see a whole manuscript, don't send a partial one. One of the first keys to success on the road to publishing is that you've got to follow the rules! You don't want to give these companies a stupid reason to reject your writing. You want them to at least read it and be impressed that you're smart enough to follow their directions.

Step 4: Create Your Proposal

After you get your guidelines and know what you're supposed to send, it's time to create a *proposal*. A proposal is a package deal that usually includes these four very important things: (1) a *cover letter* (or query), (2) your *manuscript*, (3) some *market research*, and (4) a self-addressed, stamped envelope (SASE).

Your Cover Letter

Make sure your cover letter is no more than ONE PAGE long! A great cover letter should do three things. First, it should grab an editor's attention. Make your cover letter short, interesting, and funny! Editors get pretty bored reading dozens of identical cover letters every day. Make yours stand out from the rest. Make that editor wake up and pay attention to you.

Second, your cover letter needs to summarize what your manuscript or article is about—briefly! This is not the place to write pages and pages about what they're going to soon read anyway. Keep it short and sweet—two to three sentences.

And third, your cover letter should include a little bit of information about you: any writing awards or contests you may have already won, work you do for your school newspaper or literary magazine, the inspiration for this particular piece, and even your hobbies or reasons for becoming a writer.

The next page shows an example of a great cover letter written by author Daryl Bernstein when he was a teenager. Daryl wrote this letter on his own—without help from his parents or teachers. In fact, his parents didn't even know he was submitting to publishers until his book was accepted for publication!

Your Manuscript

Once you are a hundred percent sure that the manuscript you are sending follows the requirements of the magazine or book publisher, double-check that your manuscript:

1. has a title page with your name, address, phone number, and email address in the upper right-hand corner; a word count and page count in the upper left-hand corner; and the title of your manuscript in the center of the page, with your name underneath.
2. is double-spaced. Editors like to have room to write their comments.
3. has your name and the title of your work at the top of EVERY page, just in case your title page gets lost somewhere.

Sample Query Letter

Beyond Words Publishing, Inc.
20827 N.W. Cornell Rd., Suite 500
Hillsboro, Oregon 97124-9808

Dear Beyond Words Editorial Board:

I am a fifteen-year-old honors student in Scottsdale, Arizona. I have been running my own businesses for the past five years with great success, and I am an avid *Wall Street Journal* reader.

I am interested in publishing my book *Better Than a Lemonade Stand: Small Business Ideas for Kids*. The book explains to kids of all ages how to go into small business and succeed with little or no investment or parent help.

The potential market seems excellent. The book is of interest to any kid who wants to make a buck. I have thoroughly researched the books on the subject, and have found only two in print. Both are written by adults and use language for adults rather than kids. The books are also weak on organization and provide little or no explanation of how to really start a business.

While doing my market research, I came across one of your "For Kids by Kids" books. I found the book interesting, and I felt that your publishing style will certainly appeal to kids. Although I am also considering large publishing houses, I would like to deal first with a company that has past experience in publishing for and by kids.

I am enclosing a few sample pages from my book, which is currently in progress. Please write if you are interested in publishing the book. I look forward to your response.

Sincerely,
Daryl Bernstein

4. has page numbers, in case a clumsy editor drops your stuff and pages go flying.

Remember, you can certainly get creative with your proposal, but keep in mind that multicolored paper and wacky typefaces are often more annoying than interesting. A standard-size (8 1/2 x 11) white paper, with one-inch margins all around, and a basic, read-able serif font like Times is your best bet. Let the creativity of your words and ideas grab their attention, not some hot-pink paper or gothic script.

Your Market Research

Here's where you can really get a head start on your competition. Very few writers include market research in their proposal, but publishers love it! What you want to include is one page, titled "Market Research," that describes the audience or market for your book, any similar competing books, and any unusual places a publisher could sell your book, such as specialty stores like Urban Outfitters or grocery stores like Whole Foods.

Since you've already done your homework, you should know who your market is. For submissions to magazines *and* book pub-lishers, you should write something like, "Any guy between the ages of twelve and sixteen should love my book/article on . . . ," or "Children ages four to eight and their grandparents, parents, and teachers will all enjoy reading my book/story."

The second step on your Market Research page is just for book publishers—if you're only submitting to magazines, just skip it. After listing who you think will want to buy your book, list a few other books out there that are similar to yours and *how yours is different and better*. (If no other books like yours have ever been published, good for you! Tell them that.) Maybe you wrote a book about great after-school snacks for teens. You could men-tion that other book you saw that had after-school recipes for kids, but point out that it was written for very young children while yours is written for teens. And the other after-school snack book that is written for teens is really boring and lame, but yours is hip and cool. This is where you tell the editor why your book is so important.

And last, brainstorm some ideas about where a publisher could sell your book, besides in bookstores (again, skip this step for magazines). Your after-school snack book could be sold in kitchen stores, grocery stores, and even high schools! Think outside the box; be creative. Make the publisher see how many people will love to buy your book.

Market research is the first thing book publishers do when they get a manuscript they are interested in. And even magazine editors will find your information helpful. By sending them market research with your manuscript, you're doing their homework for them! And who doesn't love it when someone does their homework for them?

> *Do your research. When possible, address your query directly to the acquisitions editor. Don't just use the editor's name from a previously published piece (he or she might not work for that publisher anymore). Look at the publisher's website, literarymarketplace.com, or writersmarket.com to get the most up-to-date contact information. (Literary Market Place and Writer's Market are updated yearly and can be found in book form at most local libraries.)*

Your SASE

You really know you're around real writers when you hear people talking about their SASEs ("say-zees"). That's because including that Self-Addressed, Stamped Envelope is such a common part of the submission process. If you want your manuscript sent back to you (just in case, for some unthinkable reason, the magazine or book publisher decides *not* to publish it), your proposal package needs to include an envelope with your name, address, and postage on it.

Your SASE *must* have enough postage on it to get back to you. If not, kiss your manuscript good-bye—companies not only won't return it to you (if they did that for everyone, they'd go broke pretty quickly!), they'll get annoyed that you didn't read their rules. Make sure that you weigh your manuscript at the post office on a letter scale so you know how much postage you need to put on your SASE. Also, a helpful tip, make sure you don't use dated postage. It won't be valid after the date printed on the postage label.

> *Do your research! If you're going for a particular publishing house, make sure your book fits in with their other titles but isn't exactly the same as one they already have. If you're looking at a magazine, make sure you know what kind of articles they publish and what subjects they're interested in.*

Step 5: Keeping Track

Once you start sending out your work, you need to keep track of where it's gone! Every time you send out a proposal, write down this information:

1. what you sent.
2. the editor and the publisher you sent it to. (If possible, it's always better to find a specific editor than just the department.)
3. the date you mailed it.
4. how much it cost to mail.
5. how long the magazine or book publisher is supposed to take to respond (this is listed in their writer's guidelines).
6. the date you get a response, plus any comments they give you.

Some writers keep a box with index cards to keep track of everything; others keep a list on their computer. Whatever works for you is fine, but do something. It's better to keep track as you go along than to try to remember later.

Step 6: The Waiting

Now's the hard part—waiting. Keep track of when your chosen

magazines and book publishers are *supposed* to respond to your proposal. If they say it takes them eight to twelve months to respond, don't start freaking out after six months! If eight months go by and you haven't heard anything, it's perfectly fine for you to give them a call or send a letter, email, or postcard to find out what's up. *Do not* call before their time is up!

Since it can take months to get a response to your proposal, and since you'll probably go crazy waiting, this is a good time to *keep writing*! Cut out the following checklist and stick it somewhere you can easily find it as you start sending out proposals (like on your bulletin board or the side of your computer), and don't forget to check it every time you send something out ... even if you *think* you remember all the steps. Better safe than sorry!

Checklist for Proposals:

My proposal includes:

1. a cover letter.
2. my manuscript, which:
   - has a title page including my name, address, phone number, and email address;
   - is double-spaced, has one-inch margins, uses a plain font, and is printed on plain white paper;
   - has been checked for spelling and grammar mistakes;
   - has page numbers, my name, and the manuscript title on each page.
3. market research.
4. a SASE.

If this all seems like a lot of work, well, you're right. It is. But look at the bright side—you have written something you want the rest of the world to see. You are definitely on your way. Just remember when you were still wondering what you would write about! You may not see your work published next month, or even next year, but if you stay with it, you will make it as a writer.

Young Author Profile:
Zoe Skye

Twenty-five-year-old **Zoe Skye** is a graduate of Columbia University and a doctoral student in English at the Graduate Center, CUNY. She works as a book reviewer.

When did you know you wanted to be a writer?
I think I always wanted to write about books—it just seemed the most interesting and natural thing to me. Realizing in middle-school and high school English that close readings and passage analyses were my favorite parts of the class...it all stemmed from that.

What do you like to write the most and why?
I'm most comfortable writing about fiction at this point, so I suppose you'd call that nonfiction on fiction. I like the mixture of critical distance and creativity that kind of writing can afford.

What are your goals for your writing future?
Every time I write a review, I realize how many holes there are in my literary background! So I guess a big goal is to broaden and deepen that base: to read more books and think and write about them.

What was your first published piece (and format) and how did you feel?
My first book review was published in the *Brooklyn Rail*, a great independent monthly paper that's willing to take chances on new

writers. It was pretty neat to see it in print, and even more so, it made me want to write another one.

Where else have you been published?
The *Los Angeles Times*, *Mother Jones*, and *The New York Times Book Review*.

Do you write full-time, and if not, would you like to? What would be your dream job?
I'm starting a graduate program in English, so soon enough I'll be writing about books full-time, in one way or another. It's hard to imagine anything I'd rather do.

What advice would you give to a young writer?
For someone who wants to review, take a chance and write to an editor: be persistent, and once you've published one review and have a clip to show for it, it'll be that much easier to write the next.

Do you think reading helps your writing?
I couldn't write a thing without reading!

What are your favorite reads?
For book reviews, I like *Bookforum*, *The New York Times Book Review*, *The Literary Review*, *The Nation*, *The Guardian*, *The Millions*, and various other newspapers, magazines, and blogs.

Name some of the authors who have inspired you and why.
Dwight Garner is one of my favorite reviewers—there's a pith and clarity to his writing that's poetic at the same time.

Getting Published: What to Do if They Say No—What to Do if They Say Yes!

Scenario #1: You rush home from school, yank open the mailbox, and . . . yes! It's a letter from a publisher! Your hands shake as you open it. Your eyes have trouble focusing, and then you read that killer first sentence: "Thank you for your recent submission; however, it does not fit our editorial needs at this time." Bummer. That's your twelfth rejection letter! You're starting to wonder if you've got what it takes to be a writer after all.

What to Do if They Say No

Be prepared: It is very, very likely that you will get rejected before you get your first piece of writing published. Next, keep it in perspective. This is part of being a writer. Welcome to the club. Every writer gets rejected at some point. But remember, it's not you that is getting rejected. If a magazine or book publisher says no to your proposal, that only means that your writing wasn't *suitable* for that particular company at that particular time. It doesn't necessarily mean your writing is no good—it could mean that an editor just published a book similar to yours or that the magazine has decided to go with a different kind of material for the next few issues.

Whatever the reason, if you have sent your very best work, don't be discouraged. Rejection doesn't mean you don't have talent. If you are serious about getting your work published and are willing to do the homework, you *will* succeed. Keep sending out those proposals and keep on writing. Your day will come.

Also keep in mind that just because your story didn't work for an editor in November, it may be just what she's looking for in May. Keep an eye on the market and on their staff. If you are determined your piece is right for that magazine or publishing house, you may try resubmitting if current events line up to better showcase the timeliness of your idea. And you can always send your story to a different editor who has never seen it before. Times change … and so do editors and their interests. So don't give up.

What to Do When if Say Yes

Scenario #2: The phone rings and you pick it up. It's an editor from your favorite magazine, asking, "Is Megan there?" Your fingers go numb and it takes all your strength to keep from dropping the phone. Your knees start to buckle and your voice shakes as you squeal, "Yes, I'm Megan!" The editor says, "We'd like to use the manuscript you sent us." You practically faint! It's your dream come true.

Don't drop the phone and *do* sit down! This could be your reality. When your writing is finally accepted for publication, it will surely be one of the most exciting moments of your life.

Besides staying cool, calm, and collected, what are you supposed to do if your dreams come true and they say yes? If you work hard and do get something accepted for publication, there are a few things you should know about the business side of writing.

When a magazine or book publisher agrees to publish your work, the first thing that will happen is that you will receive a contract to sign. When you see that first contract, you may say, "It's all Greek to me," but the good news is that legalese (the legal language that contracts are written in) will get easier for you to understand the more you get published.

Contracts and Getting Paid

The rules of contracts and payment are different for magazines and books, so we'll describe both.

Magazine Contracts

Magazines will pay you one time for using your writing. But not all magazines (and especially those that feature writing for kids) pay for writing in *dollars and cents*. Instead, they may send you some free copies of the issue in which your article, story, or poem appears. Or they might give you a year's subscription to the magazine.

Beware!

A vanity press is a company that agrees to publish your book for you, but you have to pay *them*, instead of the other way around. There are vanity presses out there that will even send you flattering letters or emails about your writing and invite you to have your writing in their next anthology of "outstanding young writers." The book may actually get published, but it will cost you a "small fee."

While you may be interested in this kind of publishing, make sure you know exactly what your fee will be and what that fee pays for *before* you agree to anything. Never sign a vanity press contract without getting experienced advice first. Some of these publishers are wonderful, others are not.

There are also plenty of websites that will post your writing. Some of these work like vanity presses: you pay us, we post your writing. Again, that's not necessarily a bad thing, but be careful and read the fine print before you send them any money. And no matter what, it is best *not* to give your real name, address, school, or telephone number over the internet.

If a magazine does pay you money for your writing, you will either get paid "on publication" or "on acceptance." Getting paid on publication means you'll get paid when your writing appears in the magazine. If your writing is accepted in March and the magazine plans to print your writing in the December issue, you'll get paid in December. Getting paid on acceptance is exactly what it sounds like—you get paid when the magazine agrees to buy your work. This kind of payment information should be in the writer's guidelines that you sent away for. (You did that, right?)

Take a look at the sample magazine contract on the next page. It's fairly simple—not too much legal mumbo jumbo!

Book Contracts

Book contracts are usually a lot longer than magazine contracts. If you receive a book contract, you should definitely go over it with someone who knows something about contracts and legalese (a literary agent is good for this and will normally consult if you don't wish to use their services for negotiations) and have them explain it all to you. Always make sure you completely understand what you are signing. Each book publisher has different payment arrangements, just like magazines. For example, some publishers pay a flat fee, which means they pay you just once, like magazines. But most book publishers pay what are called *royalties*.

Royalties (hey, you get to be the king or queen here!) are what the publisher pays you in exchange for you letting them publish your writing. A royalty is a percentage of the cover price for every book the publisher sells. That percentage can vary anywhere from 2 percent to 20 percent and will be listed in your contract. So, if a publisher charged $10 for your book and you got a 10 percent royalty, you would get $1 for each book they sold. Got it? When you get to the royalty section of the contract, get out that calculator.

Royalty checks are usually paid a few times a year and continue as long as your book keeps selling. Sometimes a publisher will pay you what is called an *advance*. An advance is a payment the publisher makes to you *before* your book is in the stores. It's not extra money, just part of your royalties that they pay you up

Sample Contract

Author's Agreement

I, (author's name) of (address), for and in consideration of the sum of (amount $_____), and other good and valuable consideration hereby sell, transfer, assign, and convey to (name of publisher), a corporation located at (publisher address), all my right, title, and interest in the work, (name of article) for the (month/year) issue, including but not limited to the right to copyright and publish and otherwise use the property in any way that said (company name) in its sole judgment shall determine.

I hereby warrant and represent that I am the sole copyright owner and proprietor of the work and that the work is not in the public domain, will not infringe or violate any copyright, trademark, or personal or proprietary rights of any person or entity, and will not contain any material which is defamatory, libelous, obscene, or otherwise in violation of the law. I also warrant and represent that I have full power and authority to enter into this Agreement. I shall indemnify and hold harmless (company name) from any and all costs and expenses (including reasonable attorney's fees) arising from any claims, suits, judgments, or settlements arising from a breach or alleged breach of my obligations, representations, and warranties herein. The foregoing representations, warranties, and indemnities shall survive any termination of this Agreement.

I have executed this assignment at_____on the_____day

of _____, 2012

Signature_____

Social Security Number_____

front. If a publisher gives you a $1,000 advance, they will deduct that from your later royalty payments. Getting an advance means that a publisher is pretty confident that your book is going to sell well. Stephen King gets huge advances because everything he writes is almost guaranteed to sell millions of copies. First-time authors, on the other hand, usually don't get paid advances. And some smaller publishers never pay advances because they operate on smaller budgets.

Know Your Rights

Magazines

Literary journals and magazine guidelines will tell you what kind of *rights* they are buying when you agree to let them publish your work. Rights? What are rights? If you write something, you are legally the owner of that material—you own the rights to it. When a magazine buys your work, it usually asks to "buy all rights." That means that you, the author, are selling your rights to the material; you no longer own what you have written. In other words, if you sell "all rights" to one of your stories to *Teen* magazine, don't even think of trying to re-sell it to *Cosmo Girl*! That's illegal!

Don't worry too much about selling all rights. That's what most first-time authors do when they're starting out. As you get published more and develop a name for yourself as an author, you will be in a better position to ask for more rights. Sometimes a magazine only wants *first serial rights*, or *one-time rights*, which means they only want the right to publish your work once, and then all rights are returned to you. With that kind of deal, you may be able to sell the same story to a different magazine or book publisher later.

Even if you sell all rights to a magazine, if you contact them after the piece has been published and ask for your rights back, often they'll agree. When you're starting out as a writer, getting those first few pieces published is the most important thing. Editors are more impressed if you've been published before—they're more likely to read your proposal more carefully. So, in the beginning, don't worry so much about how much you're going to get paid and what rights you can keep. You can haggle about all that when you're a famous writer.

Books

Book contracts also specify which kinds of rights they want to buy from you and what kind of royalty (if any) you'll be paid for each. The same rules apply as for magazines: be sure to understand what you're selling and make sure you feel like you're getting a fair deal. Again, it's best to have a lawyer or knowledgeable adult go over the rights section of the contract with you.

Working with an Editor

Once your work has been accepted and your contract is signed, an editor will begin working with you on your manuscript. Yes, even after all your careful writing and rewriting, chances are that your work will be edited again before it goes to print. *Everyone* gets edited, even famous writers, and a good editor usually makes your work even better. But working with editors can be a fun experience and should improve your writing—that's their job, after all.

Good editors help you fine-tune your ideas and words even more than you already have. And good authors are open to suggestions and excited to make their writing the best it can be. Editors and writers are like the two wheels on a bike—they work better together than alone! To give you an idea of just what an editor does, here is an example of a paragraph from this very book, before and after editing. Better, right? We thought so too!

Does this sound familiar? Lots of writers know they want to write or feel like ~~they~~ writing but just can't get started for some reason. The fact is, the hardest part ~~is often~~ just touching that pen or pencil to paper, or ~~turning on the~~ computer. Once you ~~have started~~ ~~to write~~, you are a writer. ~~Tell~~ yourself that no one needs to read ~~this, and that~~ the important thing is just to get ~~words on paper~~. It doesn't really matter what comes out ~~most~~ ~~real~~ writers admit that they write tons of junk, but that's where they find the good stuff that turns into their best writing. Here are some suggestions to help you get started.

(Hint: Turn off the television first!)

[Handwritten editor's marks: "Needs a clearer introduction about the "write" time, tools & turf." "mysterious" "new paragraph of writing can be" "typing that first word" "actually start scribbling or typing real words," "Remind" "what you're writing" "it down" "italic" "at first" "later"]

For children's and photography books, keep in mind that many publishers like to choose the illustrators/photographers, so sample illustrations/photos may not be required (unless you want to be hired as an illustrator or photographer).

This Is Your Last Chance

Once you and your editor have a final manuscript completed, you should get a final copy to review one last time. Not all publishers, especially the big ones, remember to do this. So make sure to ask your editor for last review before it goes off to the printer. This is *not* the time for you to rewrite whole pages—it's too late for that! It's also *not* the time to worry about grammar mistakes. Point any out that you happen to notice, but a professional proofreader should catch those.

This *is* the time for you to make sure you are happy with the final edits that have been made to your book and to make sure they haven't changed any facts in a way that would make them untrue or inaccurate. Read over your copy carefully and then send it back to the editor with any changes you find, marked in ink.

And More Waiting

After your last review of the book, it's time to be patient—it's tough but necessary. There is no average when it comes to how much time passes between when your work is accepted and when you finally see it in print, but a year is not unusual, even for a magazine article. For a book, it can sometimes take several years to see the final product! Believe us, it is worth the wait! Just don't start running to your mailbox as soon as you've sent off your final corrections.

The Grand Finale: Your First Book Signing

After all your work writing and editing, and after all your patient waiting, your book will finally get published and show up in bookstores. Pretty exciting! But even more exciting is when you get to do your first book signings and interviews. This is called *publicity.* You may be nervous about this aspect of being a writer, and that's totally normal. But remember, publicity helps sell your book (which means more royalties for you!) and lets you meet the people who are reading your work: your fans! Not only do you get to see your name in print, you may even make it onto the *Today* show (or at least get an interview in your local paper!). And what a great feeling to have a total stranger say to you, "I just *loved* your book. You're such a fabulous writer. Can you autograph my copy, please?"

We talked in this chapter about what happens if you get a magazine article or a book published, but the reality is that if you decide you want be a writer, you will probably write lots of different things. You will write a million cover letters, that's for sure. But it's worth it. No matter how many times your writing is published, every time you see the finished product you feel just as excited as the first time. Seeing your words in print never gets old!

And just as you can try many different kinds of writing, you can also try many different kinds of writing careers. You may start out writing novels and then move on to writing a screenplay when Hollywood decides to turn your bestseller into a movie. Or you may work as an ace reporter covering news in Europe or as a sports writer for ESPN. There are tons of exciting writing careers just waiting for you!

Young Author Profile:
Matthew (Mattie)
J.T. Stepanek

Mattie Stepanek was an American poet who had six books of poetry and one book of essays all reach the *New York Times* bestsellers list. Despite suffering from a rare form of muscular dystrophy that ended his life just before his fourteenth birthday, Mattie accomplished more than many people do in a much longer lifetime. At age three, Mattie started to write poetry as a means of coping with the death of his older brother. He appeared on *The Oprah Winfrey Show, Larry King Live*, and *Good Morning America*, acted as Muscular Dystrophy Association National Goodwill Ambassador, and became a motivational speaker and lobbyist on Capitol Hill on behalf of peace, people with disabilities, and children with life-threatening conditions.

His last book, *Just Peace: A Message of Hope*, was awarded the IPPY Gold Medal for Peacemaker Book of the Year. His funeral was attended by friends affected by his work, including Oprah Winfrey. Jimmy Carter delivered his eulogy.

We were lucky enough to talk to Mattie when he was eleven years old:

What kind of writer are you?

Mostly I write things that combine what I feel in my heart and my spirit with what I know in my head. I guess you could call much of what I write my philosophy on life. A lot of my work is poetry, but I also write short stories and essays on many different topics, and I always keep a journal. Some of my poems and stories are funny or silly. Some of them are about difficult or sad things, like when my brother died, or what it's like living with a disability, or how it felt to go through a divorce. Sometimes I write because a marvelous idea pops into my head and it becomes a story. I make an outline of chapters, then I just go and write and write and write. Other times, I might feel emotionally down about something, or excited, or angry, or confused, or thankful. Whatever my feeling is, it helps to write about how it is affecting me.

What advice do you have for other kid writers?

If you are having a difficult time coming up with something to write about, start by describing something in an unusual way. For example, look outside and describe a tree, without mentioning words like *green*, *brown*, *branches*, or *leaves*. Describe how it makes you feel or think. Describe what it sounds like. Describe how it smells. Describe a memory that it makes you think about. You can describe people, places, objects, all kinds of things. Use all of your senses, especially the ones that you wouldn't typically associate with what you are describing. The grammar and spelling and spacing can all come later. The most important thing is to get your unique ideas out. Use a tape recorder and then transcribe it, or dictate your thoughts to someone else if the actual mechanics of writing are difficult or tiresome. But get your ideas and thoughts and feelings into words, and capture them . . . for yourself and for others.

Do you ever get writer's block? If so, what helps you get through it?

Like most people, I do get writer's block. Sometimes I think it's because I have too much on my mind at certain times or because I am trying too hard to write about a certain topic. When this happens, I slow down and spend more time just writing in my journal. I might just describe a thought or a smell, or list my favorite activities or TV shows. When I relax and just begin writing about what I see, hear, feel, or think, the words begin to come easily. Then I can go back and take one of my journal entries to create a poem, essay, or short story based on what I wrote.

What is your favorite thing about writing?

My favorite things about writing are that I get to use my imagination and that I am able to share my philosophy and "Heartsongs" with other people. I always enjoy writing. No matter how I am feeling, writing makes me feel better. It helps me calm down when I am upset, it helps me give thanks and celebrate when I am happy, and it helps me organize my creativity when I have a good idea.

Here is a selection from Mattie's extensive poetry collection:

About Wishing

Some people think that
Wishing is childish.
But wishing is
For everybody.
Wishing can help the
Old feel young, and
Wishing can help the
Young grow into the
Wisdom of age.
Wishing is not
Prayer or magic,
But somewhere in between.
Like prayer and magic,
Wishing brings optimism,
And wishing brings hope.
And like prayer and magic,
Wishing brings new ideas,
And sometimes,
The touch of new life.
And that, is essential
For our future.

10

Writing as a Career: You Mean I Can Get Paid for That?

You just finished your article on the World Series for Sports Illustrated, *and now you have to dash over to the library to read a passage from your new book,* Another Perfect Storm, *to a group of young would-be writers. Then you have to start writing a column for* Seventeen, *profiling that hot new band. And somewhere in there you must find time to start working on that new mystery you have been carrying around in your head.*

If you decide that you want be a writer and earn a living at it, be prepared . . . your parents' first reactions may include at least one of the following worries:

- You, their precious child, will wind up starving in a garret (*garret* is the fancy word people use for an artist's room in the attic).

- You will become famous and weird like Ernest Hemingway and go on dangerous adventures and keep lots of six-toed cats for company.

- You will become even flakier and more out of it than you already are.

- You will start wearing a black beret, spending your nights at smoky poetry readings, and snapping your fingers instead of clapping.

- You will write embarrassing things about your family and friends!

A good way to keep your parents calm and on your side is to tell them that you are already taking this writing thing seriously. In fact, you're even researching how to be a successful writer by reading this book! Go ahead and ask your parents for help every now and then—get their story ideas, comments on your writing, proofreading help, and advice on any contracts you get. This is a double whammy: it gets them involved and excited about your writing career and also gives you free help.

If you have discovered that writing is your passion, you're in luck, because there are more cool and exciting writing careers than you can count. But how can you find out which ones you'd like best?

How to Learn More about Writing Careers

1. Don't be shy about talking to a teacher or librarian about being a writer. Good teachers live to help kids in real ways. Tell them how you've become interested in writing and ask if they can help you find good writing contests or publishing opportunities. You could also ask them to help you choose your best piece to send out.

2. If your school has a newspaper or a literary magazine, get involved.

3. Write, email, or call your local newspaper and ask if they accept *freelance* writing—stories written by people who aren't on their newspaper staff. You may be surprised at the answers you get.

4. If you are interested in writing for TV, cable TV is a good place to learn about it. Many cable companies provide opportunities for kids to get involved in working at a real TV station: you can learn how to run cameras, editing equipment, and even how to write the shows. Check with your school about local cable TV stations and whether or not they accept student interns.

5. Do an internship at a book publishing company, a magazine, or a newspaper. Check your phone book or ask a teacher about companies in your area, then call and ask if they would be interested in having a student intern. Be sure to tell them how hardworking and passionate about writing you are. This is a great way to see behind the scenes of publishing.

6. If you want to write plays or movies, volunteer at a local theater. Even if you're not into acting, there are plenty of other theater jobs that will help you learn how to write for the stage (or the big screen).

7. Read biographies of real writers to learn what their lives are/ were like and how they got started. Get inspired!

8. Write to your favorite author or call a local writer and ask for their advice. Two young writers we know wrote letters to the author Nathaniel Philbrick and got handwritten replies explaining all about how he researched his book *In the Heart of the Sea*. Most authors really enjoy talking with young people about writing. After all, they had to start out once too. But it may take them a while to get back to you, so be patient and don't get discouraged.

9. Go to writing conferences. You can find some of these listed in market directories mentioned in the chapter on resources. Also, your teacher may be able to tell you about conferences specifically for young authors. Or you can visit the website for the Society of Children's Book Writers and Illustrators (SCBWI) at scbwi.org.

10. Start your own writing group. You can work with one person or a few, and your group members don't necessarily need to be local—you can meet regularly through the internet.

> *So, you like to write and you're good at it too, but how do you make that next step toward being a professional? Practice, practice, practice through experience. Take every opportunity you can to write or learn more about it—volunteer, job shadow, do an internship. And the more focused your experiences, the better. If you want to be a sports writer, don't volunteer for a fashion magazine; try the local sports journal or TV sports reporter first.*

Real Writers Talk about Their Careers

Screenwriter

I think screenwriting is the most fun kind of writing to do. You get to imagine a movie in your head and write it down. It's mostly action and talking, without much description. And when they shoot the film, it's even more fun to see the movie from your imagination become a real movie that everyone can see.

—*Cynthia Whitcomb*
screenwriter and winner of the Christopher Award for
her screenplay *When You Remember Me*

Poet

I like writing poetry because things occur to me while doing it, things that wouldn't have occurred to me doing something else. Poetry is condensed language, and just like condensed orange juice right out of the can (before the water is added) is a stronger version of the juice you drink, poetry is a stronger, more potent version of everyday language. Poems make the reader re-experience something in a powerful way.

—*Michael Strelow*
published poet and English professor

TV Writer

Writing for TV is very different from writing for print. For one thing, you have to learn to write "for time"—your words have to fit the pictures in the story! I wrote for the evening news and I loved working on deadline. I also liked that every day was different. Nobody cares about yesterday's news, so you are always writing about something new.

—*Vicki Hambleton*
formerly a TV news writer for more than ten years

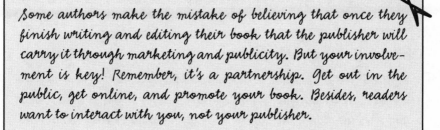

Some authors make the mistake of believing that once they finish writing and editing their book that the publisher will carry it through marketing and publicity. But your involvement is key! Remember, it's a partnership. Get out in the public, get online, and promote your book. Besides, readers want to interact with you, not your publisher.

Editor

I enjoy editing because I love decision making. I like making the choices—you are confronted with an array of possible stories and an array of possible photographs, covers . . . I love all the ingredients that go into making the magazine and putting all the pieces together. After making lots of decisions week after week as an editor, it's wonderful to take three or four weeks and dive deep into some other kind of subject and come out with a big story that may be on the cover of Time.

—*Claudia Wallis*
magazine editor and writer

Journalist

I find it amazing that I actually get paid to talk with people I find so interesting. It's fun to share stories with young readers about the people they are most interested in. My job is filled with variety and fun.

—*Janis Campbell*
newspaper feature writer for kids

Playwright

When I am writing, even though I am alone in a room, my characters keep me company. This is one reason I like to write plays: I'm never lonely. I also love to spend time around other playwrights, as well as actors, directors, and designers. Playwriting suits me because it is the perfect combination of intense solitude (while I write the play) and concentrated periods of sociability (rehearsals and performances). I have stories to tell; I have worlds to invent; I have people to create. I can't think of anything else I'd rather do.

—Bridget Carpenter
author of many plays, including *Fall*, which
won the Susan Smith Blackburn Prize in 2000

Children's Book Writer

While I was a librarian, I started thinking it would be neat to write a book. My friend Marcia and I started talking about books we liked and ones we didn't like and said, "Oh, it would be easy to do that." So the next day, we sat down for twenty minutes during our lunch break—we would eat our lunches and write at the same time. About a year and a half later, we had our first book published. I love writing for kids.

—Debbie Dadey
author of more than sixty books, including the
Adventures of the Bailey School Kids series

With the proliferation of social media, more and more readers want and expect a more intimate relationship with their favorite authors. Engage your readers online by replying to their tweets, answering emails, and providing them with exclusive content. Some authors like to post the letters and fan art they receive on their blog or other social media outlet. For ideas on how to create this relationship with your readers, follow your favorite authors online and learn from what they do.

Freelance Writer

They say necessity is the mother of invention. That also applies to the birth of my freelance career. I was about to be a single mother and writing was all I knew how to do. But sending my babies off to day-care seemed like cutting off my right arm without anesthetic. So . . . I became a freelance writer. Luckily, a WORKING freelance writer. I started writing primarily (80 percent) for children's markets. Now it's about 50/50 children's/adult markets. I love my job because of the vast flexibility of subject matter. It's as if I'm always learning, always taking new steps forward, intellectually. The "Freelance University" offers one of the best and most diverse educations on the planet.

— *Kelly Milner Halls*
freelance writer

Types of Writing Careers

Here's a list of different careers that you might want to think about:

Novelist
Sports writer
News writer for TV or radio
Foreign correspondent
Freelance writer
Editor
Fashion reporter
Medical writer
Technical writer
Screenwriter
Playwright
Children's writer
Speechwriter
Blogger

These are just some of the careers open to writers—there are many more. If you know a writer whom you admire, don't be afraid to get in touch with him or her. Ask them what they like about their job and how they got started. Many writers enjoy talking to aspiring authors and giving them encouragement. Partly that's because most writers really love what they do. There is nothing better than doing something that makes you feel happy and fulfilled (okay, and TALENTED) . . . and maybe someday even makes you rich and famous. Like anything else, a writing career takes work, but if you follow the examples in this book, you'll be well on your way to any writing career you choose!

For many careers you need years of training, but the great thing about being a writer is that you can do it at any age. You don't have to finish college or pass a bunch of tests before you can start. You can also change your form, style, and the market for your writing as often as you like. If you start out writing sci-fi/fantasy, you are not stuck with it for life—there are plenty of other genres out there! And if you start out writing magazine articles, you can easily move on to writing novels too. The more you live and have different experiences, the more you will have to write about!

Your Life as a Writer

You're humming to yourself on the school bus, of all places, and your cheeks kind of hurt from all that smiling. You can't wait to get home and get this into your journal—and maybe try a new writing prompt too. It was pretty amazing today when Mrs. Crabapple gave out copies of this month's Teen Ink *in English and your short story was in it. There it was, your writing, and there was your name, in print. The whole class cheered. You know that not only do you want be a writer—you are a writer!*

So, you want be a writer? Go for it! Look over this book and start anywhere you want—set up your writing space, get yourself a journal, try a new writing prompt, order a book, start a writing group, read a magazine with writing by young authors—these things that real writers do, and lots more, are right here for you. We said in the first chapter that, if you like to write, you are one of the luckiest people in the world, and we meant it. It's something you can do right now, do for the rest of your life, love every minute of—and even get paid for! See ya in print!

Stacy Cortigiano, Copy Editor

Stacy Cortigiano is thirty-two years old. She is a graduate of the University of Connecticut, with a bachelor's degree in English literature.

When did you know you wanted to be a copy editor?

As an undergraduate, I worked as an office assistant in the English department. One day I spotted a posting for publishing internships. I've written stories for as long as I could write, but I had never considered other aspects of publishing. I already had a small child to support, so the idea of being a struggling writer wasn't appealing. I had no idea what else I could do with the English degree I would be earning in a few semesters (I knew I didn't want to teach). The revelation that I could feed my son by helping other people with their writing was a happy accident. I was already rather compulsive about writing and grammar. It seemed like copyediting would be a perfect fit, and it has been.

What does a copy editor do?

A copy editor is responsible for perfecting what someone else has written. A good copy editor goes entirely unnoticed. If you read something with mistakes in it—typos, factual errors, grammatical errors, inconsistent phrasing and styling—the copy editors didn't do their job well (or—gasp!—it wasn't copyedited at all).

How is copyediting related to writing? Did you ever want to be a writer?

I've written stories for as long as I can remember. To be a good copy editor, you have to be a good writer. You have to have an

159

innate grasp of the mechanics of writing (grammar, structure, diction—all relating to a fiction or nonfiction topic that people want to read). The reason writers can't copyedit their own work is because they can't be impartial about it. They've stared at their own words for too long and can't see the mistakes and inconsistencies. That's why good copy editors are invaluable.

What was your first copyediting job?
The internship I did in college turned into my first copyediting job. It was a small book publisher and packager in northeast Connecticut. That's where I learned about *The Chicago Manual of Style*, how to make style sheets, and how to use design programs.

What are your goals for your literary future?
I'm only thirty-two, but I've already had eleven years of experience as a copy editor. I'm the Senior Copy Editor of the copyedit team at the publisher I work for. My goal has been to be heavily involved in creating the policies and procedures for my team while still spending most of my time copyediting, and I've accomplished that. I'm happy where I am, doing what I do. I still write when an idea strikes me.

What advice would you give to a young writer interested in copyediting?
My advice would be to read good books and pay close attention to them. The internet is wonderful for many things, but it is not a paragon of writing proficiency. Also, take a copyediting class. They're usually associated with journalism programs at colleges. And figure out which type of copyediting you're interested in and learn the style manual of that sub-field. Book publishing and many magazines use *Chicago*. Newspapers and other magazines use the *AP Style Guide*. There's a separate style guide for medical writing.

Do you think reading helps you with your job?
I started reading classic literature when I was twelve. I absorbed

a lot of proper writing technique by osmosis. The classics are still my books of choice.

What are your favorite reads?
I mainly stick to the academic canon, but I read some living writers too. I read a lot of news on the internet. I'm happy if e-readers have gotten more people into reading, but I stick with paper-and-ink books.

Name some of the authors who have inspired you and why.
J. D. Salinger, E. L. Doctorow, Virginia Woolf, William Shakespeare, Joyce Carol Oates, Thomas Hardy, F. Scott Fitzgerald, Ralph Ellison, Edith Wharton, Charles Dickens, Leo Tolstoy, Fyodor Dostoevsky, Jane Austen, the Brontës, Herman Melville, Nathanial Hawthorne, Henry James, Theodore Dreiser, William Faulkner, Mark Twain, T. S. Eliot. Their writing is beautiful and thought-provoking, as the best writing should be.

11

Resources for Writers

Maybe you know writers who can just sit down and write every day with no problems, but we don't! Most writers do lots of things to get their creative juices flowing, including taking writing courses, joining writing groups, reading books about writing, and using writing prompts for inspiration. Here are some of the wonderful books available that are particularly good for young writers. We have also given you some suggestions for different contests you can enter and magazine and book publishers that are interested in the writing of young adults. You'll find everything you need to know, from contacts to websites to addresses!

Get More Information on How to Be a Better Writer

The Elements of Style, 4th edition. William Strunk Jr. and E. B. White. Whiteplains, NY: Longman, 1999.

This classic grammar and style reference book, penned by a university professor in 1918, is still indispensable for many writers today. It includes tips on how to write well and lists of commonly misused and misspelled words.

Getting the Knack: 20 Poetry Writing Exercises. Stephen Dunning and William Stafford. Urbana, IL: National Council of Teachers of English, 1992.

These two authors are very respected contemporary poets, and their book describes fun and interesting forms of poetry, like pantoums and acrostics, as well as wonderful techniques and prompts that can be used for other kinds of writing besides poetry.

Grammar Girl: grammar.quickanddirtytips.com

Mignon Fogarty explains grammar in a fun, easily understandable way. Whether you want to look up a particular rule or just browse the archives for tips to improve your writing, this site is a must-visit.

Grammar Smart: A Guide to Perfect Usage, 2nd edition. Jeff Soloway, ed. New York: Princeton Review Publishing, 2001.

All writers need and deserve a good grammar handbook.

Live Writing: Breathing Life into Your Words. Ralph Fletcher. New York: Avon Books, 1999.

Fletcher gives practical tips and suggestions that fit all kinds of writers, at all kinds of stages of their writing lives.

MIT OpenCourseWare: ocw.mit.edu

This Massachusetts Institute of Technology program allows anyone to download course materials and exercices for many college subjects, including writing courses. If you're looking for more advanced exercises or just want a taste of what college writing classes might be like, this website is a good way to find out.

The Place My Words Are Looking For: What Poets Say About and Through Their Work. Paul B. Janeczko, ed. New York: Simon & Schuster Books for Young Readers, 1990.

Thirty-nine of our leading poets share their poetry as well as their thoughts, inspirations, anecdotes, and memories. The poems are beautifully crafted, clear, and on a variety of subjects for all kinds of young adult readers. Each poet writes a few paragraphs about his or her writing and about what life is like for a writer—a unique source of ideas about writing by real writers.

READ: weeklyreader.com/read

From Weekly Reader Corporation this monthly magazine is for young readers and writers in grades 6–10. It has stories, plays, and poems, plus articles about writers and writing. The magazine encourages readers to send in their writing for possible publication and sponsors annual writing contests (word@ weeklyreader.com).

Scope: scholastic.com

A monthly magazine for readers and writers in grades 6–9. It includes articles on current events and movies, followed by interesting writing prompts and opportunities to send your writing to contests in the magazine. Contact Scholastic Inc., 555 Broadway, New York, NY 10012-3999 or scopemag@ scholastic.com.

Sleeping on the Wing: An Anthology of Modern Poetry with Essays on Reading and Writing. Kenneth Koch and Kate Farrell. New York: Vintage Books, 1982.

An excellent collection of famous poets and their poems. You will learn how the poets got their ideas and about their techniques. Best of all, the book includes prompts for writing poems or stories based on some of the famous pieces.

The Teachers and Writers Handbook of Poetic Forms, 2nd edition. Ron Padgett, ed. New York: Teachers & Writers, 2000.

Lists poetic forms alphabetically and includes a clear definition and description of each, plus poets who write in that form and sample poems.

Writers Inc: A Student Handbook for Writing and Learning. Patrick Sebranek, Dave Kemper, and Vernel Meyer. Wilmington, MA: Great Source Education Group, 2011.

This easy-to-use and very comprehensive book has short, clear definitions and explanations for all areas of writing, including grammar and usage, plus standard formats and content for different forms of writing. This is a book a writer can use in middle school, high school, college, and beyond.

A Writer's Notebook: Unlocking the Writer Within You. Ralph Fletcher. New York: Avon Books, 1996.

This guide will show you exactly how to keep a writer's notebook, the most important tool a writer can have.

Writing Smart, 2nd edition. Marcia Lerner. New York: Princeton Review Publishing, 2001.

This is a basic guide to writing that you can use as a reference for various forms and formats, as well as methods for citations, bibliography, and so on.

Writing to Deadline: The Journalist at Work. Donald M. Murray. Portsmouth, NH: Heinemann, 2000.

If you are interested in nonfiction writing, this is the book for you. This books lets you into the real life of the journalist.

Writing toward Home: Tales and Lessons to Find Your Way. Georgia Heard. Portsmouth, NH: Heinemann Boynton/Cook, 1995.

Over fifty-five different and fascinating writing prompts. By the time you finish reading just one of these prompts, you'll be itching to write.

Writing with Power: Techniques for Mastering the Writing Process. Peter Elbow. New York: Oxford University Press, 1981.

Elbow is a famous writing teacher who gives readers lists of great writing topics and ideas for expanding their writing after they've gotten started.

Writing Your Own Plays: Creating, Adapting, Improvising. Carol Korty. New York: Players Press, 2000.

This book gives you practical tips and helpful examples to improve your playwriting skills.

Yoga for the Brain: Daily Writing Stretches That Keep Minds Flexible and Strong. Dawn DiPrince and Cheryl Miller Thurston. Fort Collins, CO: Cottonwood Press, Inc., 2006.

This contains 365 interesting writing prompts for teens, one for every day of the year.

Get More Information on How to Get Published

Kid Magazine Writers: kidmagwriters.com

Aimed at helping both teens and adults writing for children's magazines, this website keeps a thorough, up-to-date list of kid magazines that accept submissions, plus links to their guidelines.

2012 Novel and Short Story Writer's Market. Adria Haley, ed. Cincinnati, Ohio: Writer's Digest Books, 2011.

2012 Poet's Market. Robert Lee Brewer, ed. Cincinnati, Ohio: Writer's Digest Books, 2011.

2012 Writer's Market. Robert Lee Brewer, ed. Cincinnati, Ohio: Writer's Digest Books, 2011.

These directories are updated and issued in a new volume each year and are available at public libraries and bookstores. Used by serious writers to locate all kinds of publishers and submission information, they contain thousands of listings of publishers, contests, and awards, as well as complete submission and contact information. *Writer's Market* also publishes a monthly magazine. In addition, the creators' website (writersdigest.com) has forums, blogs, writing tips and prompts, contests, and guidelines to getting published.

"Get Your Students' Work Published." Horace Mann Educators Corporation. Reach Every Child, http://reacheverychild.com/feature/kids_publish.html.

Although this site was made for teachers who want to help their students get published, you can help yourself to this list of magazines and websites that publish writing by kids and teens.

Go Public! Encouraging Student Writers to Publish. Susanne Rubenstein. Urbana, IL: NCTE, 1998.

Although *Go Public!* is intended for middle and high school teachers, it is a handy reference guide to publishing opportunities, especially the chapters titled "The Market and Contest Lists" and "Electronic Submissions." Visit ncte.org.

Screenwriting for Teens: The 100 Principles of Screenwriting Every Budding Writer Must Know. Christina Hamlett. Studio City, CA: Michael Wiese Productions, 2006.

Aimed at those who aspire to write their own films, this guide includes the basics of screenwriting, the business side of the process, mental exercises, writing exercises, and a recommended reading (and viewing) list.

A Teen's Guide to Getting Published, 2nd edition. Jessica Dunn and Danielle Dunn. Waco, TX: Prufrock Press, Inc., 2006.

Written by two authors who were first published as teens, this book offers an introduction to the business of writing, as well as lists of print and online publishers that accept the work of young writers. There is also information about contests and writers' camps.

Get Your Writing Published

You've gotta be in it to win it! Send your writing to a few of these places to see yourself in print. Magazines will send you a free copy if you are published in a printed issue. The hardcover anthologies will send you information on how to purchase a copy of the book, but the anthologies listed here do *not* obligate you to purchase the book in order to be included in the book.

Magazines and e-zines

The Apprentice Writer (grades 9–12). Short stories, personal experience essays, profiles, poems, and photo essays are all published in this annual. It is distributed to schools in the middle Atlantic states. Contact: Writers Institute Director, Susquehanna University, 610 University Avenue, Selinsgrove, PA 17870-1164. Web: susqu.edu.

Bookworm (grades 5–8). *Bookworm* magazine publishes the stories, poems, essays, and artwork of kids ages six through fifteen. It is edited by Sophie McKibben, who founded the magazine in 2004 when she was in sixth grade and noticed that there weren't a lot of places for kids to get their work into print. *Bookworm* comes out four times a year and has featured the writing and art of kids from all over the United States and, so far, five foreign countries. *Bookworm* is always on the lookout for writers and artists. You can submit your work electronically to bookworm.mag@gmail.com.

Cicada (ages 14–21). This magazine comes out six times a year and features fiction and book reviews for young adults. Stories from readers are welcome. Contact: Submissions Editor, *Cicada*, 70 East Lake Street, Suite 300, Chicago, IL 60601. Web: cicadamag.com.

The Claremont Review (ages 13–19). A literary journal targeted for young adult writers in North America. Fiction, poetry, and short plays are judged according to maturity of content and evidence of meticulous editing. Contact: *The Claremont Review*, 4980 Wesley Road, Victoria, BC, Canada V8Y 1Y9. Web: theclaremontreview.ca.

Creative Kids (ages 8–14). An opportunity for children to share their creative and expressive work in a publication that is read by thousands of readers. Contact: Submissions Editor, *Creative Kids*, P.O. Box 8813, Waco, TX 76714-8813. Web: http://prufrock.com/client/client_pages/prufrock_jm_createkids.cfm.

Cricket (ages 6–16). A different contest is announced in each month's issue. Genres vary: poetry, short story, nonfiction, art. Contact: Submissions Editor, *Cricket*, 70 East Lake Street, Suite 300, Chicago, IL 60601. Web: cricketmag.com.

Cyberteens (age 19 and younger). Teen writers and artists are featured on this e-zine. Stories, articles, poems, opinion pieces, and reviews of software, books, and music are all found on the site. Email: editor@cyberteens.com, web: cyberteens.com.

Girls' Life (girls ages 10–15). This bimonthly magazine is available in libraries and stores and accepts all kinds of articles written by girls. Contact: Editor, *Girls' Life* Magazine, 4529 Harford Road, Baltimore, MD 21214. Email: letters@girlslife .com, web: girlslife.com

KidSpirit Magazine. This online magazine publishes articles, reviews, poetry, and artwork by teens. Contact: KidSpirit Online, 77 State Street, Brooklyn, NY 11201. Email: info@kidspiritonline .com, web: kidspiritonline.com

Literary Cavalcade (grades 9–12). Features articles and stories about contemporary literature, as well as showcase student writing. Contact: Scholastic Inc., 555 Broadway, New York, NY 10012. Web: scholastic.com/writeit.

New Moon Girls (girls ages 8–14). This bimonthly magazine is edited by and for girls and accepts letters, poems, stories, drawings, and jokes written by girls. Contact: NMGM, P.O. Box 161287, Duluth, MN 55816. Phone: 218-728-5507, email: submissions@ newmoon.com, web: newmoon.com.

Pine Tree Poetry (grades 6–12). This is a very nice hardcover anthology of student poetry published once a year. Web: pinetreepoetry.com.

Polyphony H. S. This student-run national literary magazine for high school writers publishes poetry, fiction, and creative nonfiction. Contact: *Polyphony H.S.*, 1514 Elmwood Avenue, Suite 2, Evanston, IL 60201. Email: info@polyphonyhs.com, web: polyphonyhs.com.

Scholastic Scope (ages 12–19). Each issue includes an essay written by a kid about "the book that had a big effect on you." It also has a regular "Yes/No" column debating both sides of controversial topics, and contests based on writing prompts that appear after articles. Readers are encouraged to send in opinions for publication in later issues. Contact: *Scholastic Scope*, 555 Broadway, New York, NY 10012-3999. Email: scopemag@scholastic.com, web: scholastic.com.

Skipping Stones (ages 8–16). This magazine welcomes articles on different cultures as well as fiction written by young authors. Contact: Managing Editor, *Skipping Stones*, P.O. Box 3939, Eugene, OR 97403-0939. Email: editor@skippingstones.org, web: skippingstones.org.

Speak Up Press (ages 13–19). This online teen literary journal features fiction, nonfiction, and poetry by teens. They also accept book-length young adult nonfiction submissions. *Speak Up Press* is guided by an advisory board of teens who help decide on content. Email: submit@speakuppress.org, web: speakuppress.org.

Sports Illustrated for Kids (ages 8–14). This monthly magazine uses opinion pieces written by young authors. Contact: Letters, *Sports Illustrated for Kids*, email: kidletters@sikids.com, web: sikids.com.

Stone Soup (ages 8–13). Poetry, book reviews, artwork, and stories from contributors under the age of 14 are found in each issue of this magazine. Contact: *Stone Soup* Submissions Dept., P.O. Box 83, Santa Cruz, CA 95063. Email: editor@stonesoup.com, web: stonesoup.com.

Teen Ink (grades 7–12). *Teen Ink* publishes fiction, poetry, nonfiction, reviews, and interviews in their monthly newsprint magazine, quarterly poetry magazine, and on their website *Teen Ink RAW*— the largest site for young writers in the world. Send submissions to Teen Ink, P.O. Box 30, Newton, MA 02461. Email: editor@ teenink.com, web: teenink.com.

Teen Voices (girls ages 12–19). This magazine is published quarterly by a multicultural volunteer group of teens and young adult women, and contains writing by and for young women to "provide an intelligent alternative to glitzy, gossipy, fashion-oriented publications that too often exploit the insecurities of their young audiences." Female readers are encouraged to submit all forms of writing. Contact: *Teen Voices*, P.O. Box 120-027, Boston, MA 02112-0027. Phone: 617-426-5505, email: teenvoices@ teenvoices.com, web: teenvoices.com.

Word. The official blog of *READ* magazine, *Word* offers young writers opportunities to get published, make connections with books and authors, get writing tips, participate in ongoing interactive stories, and read "musings and ramblings and cool links." Web: readandwriting.com.

Write It! This is Scholastic's website for young writers. Publish your work, chat with fellow writers, build your own portfolio, and join a master class with featured writers. Web: scholastic.com/writeit.

The Writers' Slate. This online magazine publishes poetry and prose from students in kindergarten through twelfth grade. Email: KristenWorthington@writingconference.com, web: writingconference.com.

Writing Contests

READ Magazine Poetry Contest (formerly the Ann Arlys Bowler Poetry Contest). This prestigious annual poetry contest awards cash and gift certificate prizes. Winners are nationally published in *READ* magazine and on the website. December 31 deadline. Web: weeklyreader.com.

Baker's Plays High School Playwriting Competition. This contest runs every year and is designed to showcase the work of high school playwrights. Deadline April 30. Visit bakersplays.com for contest rules and entry form. Contact: High School Playwriting Contest, Baker's Plays, 45 West 25th Street, New York, NY 10010.

Claudia Ann Seaman Awards for Young Writers. Open to all students in grades nine through twelve, these awards aim to nurture the writing community and enable young writers to reach a wider audience. Deadline April 15. Submit poems, short stories, or essays through either polyphonyhs.com or teenreads.com. For information and guidelines, go to http://polyphonyhs.com/the-claudia-ann-seaman-awards-for-young-writers.

Creative Communication (grades 6–12). This organization hosts annual contests for poetry and short essays. Winners are published in their hardcover anthologies. Web: poeticpower.com.

Letters About Literature Contest (grades 4–12). This annual national contest is sponsored by the Center for the Book in the Library of Congress. "Write a letter to an author—living or dead—explaining how the author's words changed the way you view the world . . . or yourself." December 10 deadline. Web: lettersaboutliterature.org.

Kay Snow Writing Awards. This annual contest features an award for students eighteen and younger. Deadline April. Visit willamettewriters.com for additional information and guidelines. Contact: Willamette Writers, 2108 Buck Street, West Linn, OR 97068.

National Council of Teachers of English (NCTE) Promising Young Writers Program. Ask your teacher about being nominated to participate in this prestigious program for students in grades eight and eleven. Students must submit a sample of their writing, plus write an essay on a topic selected by NCTE. Deadline February. Contact: NCTE Promising Young Writers Program, 1111 W. Kenyon Road, Urbana, IL 61801-1096. Phone: 217-328-3870, email: pyw@ncte.org, web: ncte.org.

Scholastic Writing Awards. This is the contest for young writers and artists! Students in grades seven through twelve can enter short stories, essays, dramatic scripts, poetry, science fiction, fantasy, humor, or writing portfolios. Deadlines vary by region. Register online at artandwriting.org.

Weekly Reader (ages 7–12). This magazine encourages readers to send in writing of all genres for potential publication. It also sponsors several writing contests each year. Visit http://weeklyreader.com/wr/9 for a listing of current contests or http://www.weeklyreader.com/wr/253 for more kids and teens info.

The Writing Conference, Inc. Writing Contest. The Writing Conference, Inc. sponsors writing contests for elementary, junior high/middle, and high school students. Submissions may be poems, narratives, or essays, based on a different topic each year. Deadline January. Visit http://writingconference.com/contest.htm for guidelines and an entry form. Contact: The Writing Conference, Inc., P.O. Box 664, Ottawa, Kansas 66067-0664.

Young Voices (grades K–12). This short story contest gives students a prompt and then awards prizes for the best entries in each age category. Check their website for a list of submission rules. Contact: The Young Voices Foundation, 17141 Magic Mountain Drive, Round Hill, VA 20141. Email: info@youngvoicesfoundation.org, web: youngvoicesfoundation.org.

Book Publishers
Beyond Words Publishing, Inc. The company that published this book has also published hundreds of kid authors. With

declared values that include "creativity and aesthetics nourish the soul" and "living your passion is vital," this publisher truly believes in getting young writers into print. They publish only nonfiction by young writers. Contact: Beyond Words Publishing, 20827 NW Cornell Road, Suite 500, Hillsboro, OR 97124-9808. Phone: 800-284-9673, email: submissions@beyondword .com, web: beyondword.com.

Creative With Words Publications. This company publishes anthologies of fiction and nonfiction for readers of all ages. Each anthology is based on a theme and includes material from young writers. Contact: Creative With Words Publications, P.O. Box 223226, Carmel, CA 93922. Web: creativewithwords .tripod.com.

May Davenport Publishers. This company publishes fiction for grades kindergarten through twelve. It is especially interested in material for young adult readers. Contact: May Davenport Publishers, 26313 Purissima Road, Los Altos Hills, CA 94022. Web: maydavenportpublishers.com.

Young Author Profile:
Nicholas Feitel

Twenty-four-year-old **Nicholas Feitel** began developing his writing skills in elementary, middle, and high school before going on to attend NYU's film production program.

When did you know you wanted to be a writer?
I began to write at an early age. I taught myself how to write the alphabet before the class learned, spurred on by the idea that my newly received glasses meant I would have to be a smart guy, a

writer. I started writing poetry and personal stories, egged on by my mom mostly. I never really stopped writing after I began.

What do you like to write the most and why?

I like to write what some people call personal fiction or creative nonfiction, stories from my life or stories that reflect how I feel. My goal usually in writing is to reach such a specific place in my life or in a story that it becomes universally relatable: a way of both gaining control of an unwieldy life and trying to forge connections between me and the illusory world of the reader beyond my writing.

What are your goals for your writing future?

No idea. I just feel lucky enough to do what it is (whatever that is) that I'm doing right now. To just be able to tell the stories I want to tell. My college training is in screenwriting, so I guess I'd like to do more of that.

What was your first published piece (and format) and how did you feel?

Ha. My first published piece was a poem I wrote about Martin Luther King when I was about eight. It was published in a children's magazine. I remember feeling very strange about the whole ordeal, and no one in the elementary-school world of New York City really caring, except for, of course, my mom and grandma. And maybe my dad.

Where else have you been published?

Gay City News as a film/arts/theater critic for about four years. A great job writing in a strange circumstance, as I do not identify as gay, though I feel like the terms we use to describe our sexuality are very limited compared to the reality of it. It felt great to be a hack critic getting paid next to nothing and getting to pitch movies I wanted to review to the very small staff of a community newspaper. I was also a contributing editor for *FilmLinc* and now on Bethenny Frankel's site, writing food blogs. Also, occasionally, I write on Bravo's site, about dating, which I find fun.

Do you write full-time, and, if not, would you like to? What would be your dream job?

I don't and don't know if I'm ready to. My dream job? I don't know. I feel like I'm at the point in my life where I haven't experienced enough to know what or who I want to be. I'm more about enjoying the now and trying to make fewer terrible decisions that screw up my life. I figure I'll figure it out eventually—that or cop out like everyone else and go to law school.

What advice would you give to a young writer?

I think the most important thing, generally, is to love what you're doing. Writing is one of those things like acting or being a clown or a musician that people don't get into unless they have some sort of insane compulsion to do it. Find what it is in your writing you love, work that, strengthen that strength. That's your voice. And whatever craft you learn will build on it, like that creepy eye on top of a pyramid on the back of a one-dollar bill.

Do you think reading helps your writing?

Absolutely, though I don't do enough of it. But there's certainly no way I'd ever be where I am now if I hadn't read obsessively as a child and young adult, thinking books were my only friends. In that immersion into literature, both sad and wonderful, your world and mind are expanded, and you're filled with the knowledge of so many others—their experiences, their influences. It makes you stronger. That's a nice way of putting it, but basically it's just the plot of *The Giver*.

What are your favorite reads?

I only read *The New Yorker* and *The New York Times Magazine* regularly, for publications. I have really taken lately though to a website called *Instapaper*, which lets you save articles, read them later, and "like" them, and a companion site called *Give Me Something to Read*, which is a frequently updated collection of articles liked on *Instapaper*. I find it a more interesting way to check out nonfiction.

As for books? Some I've liked are *Invisible Man* by Ralph Ellison, *Holes* by Louis Sachar, and *The Imperfectionists* by Tom Rachman.

Name some of the authors who have inspired you and why.
Calvin Trillin, because of the way he writes about food, or any other subject, enmeshed in his life and perspective. Madeleine L'Engle, for expanding the minds of youth.

12

Glossary: Words That Writers, Publishers, and Teachers Use a Lot— And What They Mean!

abstract: Cannot be touched, tasted, smelled, heard, or seen (as opposed to something concrete, which can be perceived by one of the five senses). Emotions or ideas are abstract: love, hate, envy, greed, happiness, depression, anger, revenge, confidence, evil, kindness. (ch. 5)

acrostic: A poem that spells a word or phrase vertically, based on the first letter of each line. (ch. 5)

advance: A payment from a publisher when a writer signs a contract for a book. The advance is part of a writer's royalty payment, paid up front and deducted from later royalty payments. (ch. 9)

archetype: A *model* that is used over and over in literature. One example of an archetype is the classic hero (or heroine): an unlikely hero, called upon to go on a journey, encounters dangers, gathers friends, is helped by someone older and wiser, is successful because of cleverness and goodness rather than brute strength, and returns home with a new understanding that is not always appreciated. (ch. 2)

autobiography: The story of a real person's life, written by the person herself. (ch. 3)

bibliography: A list of the sources that an author used to write a book or research paper.

biography: The story of a real person's life, written by another person. (ch. 3)

blog: Short for "web log," an online journal. (ch. 2)

call for manuscripts: An advertisement that invites writers to submit writing by a certain date, usually on a specific topic or in a specific genre. Magazines often have their call for manuscripts in the front or back pages. Publishers and magazines insert their calls in writing magazines, *Writer's Market* books, and on their websites.

character: A person (not necessarily human) who takes part in the action of a literary work. (ch. 6)

characterization: The act of creating and developing a character by (1) direct description; (2) dialogue—what the character says or what other characters say about him; and/or (3) actions—what the character does or what others do around the character. (ch. 6)

cite or citation: To cite is to include a very short note, or citation, that gives the name of an author and title of the work from which you are using words or ideas. Citation is included in the text of a writing piece and in a bibliography. (ch. 5) *climax:* The high point of interest or suspense in a story; the point at which the conflict is revealed. Some call the climax the *turning point* in a piece of writing. (ch. 6)

conflict: A struggle between opposing forces. *Internal conflict* occurs within the character's heart or mind. *External conflict* occurs between a character and an outside force: another character or a force of nature (animal, weather, flood, disease, etc.). (ch. 6)

contract: A contract is a legal agreement between a publisher and an author. (ch. 9)

cover letter: A letter that you send with your manuscript, introducing yourself and your writing. (ch. 8)

dialogue: Words said out loud in a conversation. When you write dialogue, use a book by a good author as a model for how to punctuate. (ch. 3, 5)

diary: A book in which you write about the events and ideas that occur in your life. Also called a *journal.* (ch. 2)

draft: Any piece of writing that is not ready to send to a publisher or a contest. A *rough draft* is writing in its earliest stages that you still plan to revise. A *final draft* has gone through revisions and editing so that it is finally ready to send out. Most writers number and date each draft. If you write directly on the computer, just put the date as part of the file name each time you save changes. Save hard copies of all drafts—you might use stuff you cut out in something else later on. (ch. 6,7)

editor: An editor makes suggestions to the author for additions, deletions, and reorganization in his or her writing so that it flows more logically and effectively for the reader. (ch. 8, 10) *epilogue:* A concluding section that comes after the end of a work. An epilogue often summarizes the final results in the future for most or all characters. (ch. 5)

exposition: Comes at the beginning of a piece of writing; the exposition introduces the reader to characters, setting, and conflict. An exposition is also a form of writing (expository writing) that is written to inform, compare, contrast, analyze, give cause and effect, or give how-to instructions. (ch. 6)

fable: A piece of fiction that teaches a lesson or a *moral*. Animal fables give animals human characteristics: the animals speak and act like human beings, and often show human emotions, virtues, and vices. (ch. 5) See *personification*.

found poem: A poem fashioned from someone else's writing (with the source cited). Usually, the original writing was *not* meant to be poetic, but the poet's artful choices, deletions, and rearrangement make a new kind of meaning and sense. (ch. 5)

freewriting: Writing that is meant to get ideas and thoughts on paper with no concern for spelling, punctuation, grammar, sentence structure, paragraphs, or even staying on topic. (ch. 4)

genre: Kind of writing (biography, science fiction, mystery, etc.) (ch. 2, 3)

guidelines: An explanation of a publisher's editorial needs and desires, which can include genre, subject matter, word length, and reading level. (ch. 8)

imprint: An imprint is a subdivision of a publishing company that focuses on publishing material for a specific market, such as books for teens, nonfiction, biography, and so forth.

inciting incident: An event in the beginning of a story, play, or narrative that introduces the conflict. (ch. 6)

journal: A book in which you write thoughts, observations, ideas, or anything that strikes you. Also called a *diary.* (ch. 2)

manuscript: A complete piece of original writing. Publishers and contests have guidelines for manuscripts that they publish. (ch. 8)

market: The intended audience of a piece of writing. (ch. 8)

memoir: Autobiographical writing based on the writer's memories, usually written in the first person ("I"). (ch. 3)

metaphor: A figure of speech in which one thing is spoken of as if it were something else. Example: *Happiness is a warm puppy.* (ch. 6)

model: A pattern or figure of something to be made. Writers use books, stories, plays, and authors as models for their ideas and styles. Models can also be used to answer questions about punctuating dialogue or writing a bibliography. (ch. 3, 5)

monologue: A long speech spoken by one person. (ch. 3, 5)

moral: A lesson that is usually stated directly at the end of a story. (ch. 5)

personification: The representation of a thing or an idea as a person or by the human form.

plagiarism: Using someone else's words or ideas in your writing, without giving credit to the real author. Plagiarism is a serious offense—students who plagiarize can get expelled from school, adults who plagiarize can get fired from their jobs, and authors who plagiarize can get sued. It comes from the Latin word meaning "to kidnap or abduct for ransom"—plagiarists kidnap the words of others for their own benefit. (ch. 5)

plot: A sequence of events—beginning, middle, and end—in a piece of writing. (ch. 6)

point of view: The perspective or vantage point from which a story is told. There is the first person point of view ("I"), the second person point of view ("you"—usually only found in how-to writing), and the third person point of view ("they/he/she/it"). (ch. 6, 7)

prologue: A description of characters or events that have happened before the first chapter of a story. (ch. 5)

prompt: A short lesson or a few paragraphs that are meant to stimulate you as a writer and help you get started writing something. (ch. 4, 5)

query: A query is a letter sent to a publisher that describes the proposal and outlines an author's qualifications to write the article or book. (ch. 8)

reader: Someone who reads a piece of writing and responds to it so that the writer can find out what his or her potential audience might get from a particular piece. (ch. 7)

revise: To change an earlier draft in some way that affects the content: adding or inserting, deleting, combining sentences, moving around paragraphs, and rewriting parts in new ways to decide which way the writer likes best. With each revision, the writing should get better, more organized, and more interesting. (ch. 4, 6)

rights: When a publisher buys a manuscript, they are buying the right to publish that manuscript. (ch. 9)

royalty: A publisher pays a writer a percentage of the cover price for each copy of the author's book that is sold. (ch. 9)

SASE: Self-Addressed, Stamped Envelope. An envelope that has your name, address, and enough postage on it for the publisher to return your manuscript (if you want it back), or for the publisher to send back a note saying your submission was received—or accepted! (ch. 8)

style guide: A style is a set of standards (beyond basic grammar) for the writing and design of documents. The style guide for a specific publisher is known as "house style." Formerly published style guides are called style manuals. Book publishing generally uses *The Chicago Manual of Style*. Newspapers and journals usually use *The Associated Press Stylebook*. Some other common style manuals are the *MLA Style Manual* and *The Publication Manual of the APA*.

theme: The central message an author wants to convey in his/her writing. In most literature, the theme is not directly stated but can be implied by the reader. Theme is different from a *moral*. (ch. 5)

turning point: See *climax*.

writer's guidelines: See *guidelines*.

writing group: A group of writers who meet regularly to learn about writing and share, respond to, and critique each other's writing. (ch. 7)

ABOUT THE AUTHORS

Vicki Hambleton is a professional writer, TV writer/ producer, museum docent, and tutor. She has worked for publications such as *US* magazine and *Good Housekeeping*. She founded the magazine *Parenting Teens* and created a research book for reporters, which led to research—and eventually writer and producer—positions in the Special Events division of ABC news and a position as a producer at CBS news.

Vicki currently works as a full-time tutor for high school students in addition to working as a docent at the Morgan Library and Museum in New York and continuing to write. She lives in Connecticut on a horse farm where she can often be found hiking with her Welsh corgis or riding horses.

Cathleen Greenwood is a teacher, published writer, and veteran presenter at national and local professional conferences on teaching and writing. She loves to see young writers share their writing with the world.

In addition to coauthoring her book on writing for teenagers and two books on writing for teachers, Cathy has published poems, short stories, and essays in magazines and journals such as NCTE's *English Journal* and *Council Chronicle*, NYSEC's *English Record* and *NYSEC News*, *AIM magazine*, and the *Vineyard Gazette*. She has won awards for teaching and writing from the New York State English Council, Channel Thirteen, *English Journal*, and *Teen Ink*, as well as the O'Rourke Prize for Distinguished Achievement in Curriculum Design for using the principles in the book *Using Understanding by Design* by Grant Wiggins and Jay McTighe.